RIVAL. Crock Pot®

The Original and #1 Brand Slow Cooker

Slow Cooker Recipes

for All Occasions

Publications International Ltd.

Favorite Brand Name Recipes at www.fbnr.com

Pictured on front cover: Quatro Frijoles Con Pollo Cantara (*page 77*).

Pictured on back cover: Thai Chicken (*page 54*), Maple-Glazed Meatballs (*page 36*), and Peach-Pecan Upside-Down Cake (*page 138*).

ISBN 13: 978-1-4127-2494-4
ISBN 10: 1-4127-2494-5

Manufactured in China.

8 7 6 5 4 3 2 1

Preparation/Cooking Times: Preparation times are based on the approximate amount of time required to assemble the recipe before cooking, baking, chilling, or serving. These times include preparation steps such as measuring, chopping, and mixing. The fact that some preparations and cooking can be done simultaneously is taken into account. Preparation of optional ingredients and serving suggestions is not included.

Table of Contents

What Will You Cook Up Next? **4**

Slow Cooking 101 **8**

Easy Entertaining **11**

 Impress Your Guests **12**
 Fabulous fare for every entertaining occasion

 World-Class Cuisine **54**
 Festive recipes from popular world cuisines

Beyond the Entrée **93**

 Spectacular Sides **94**
 Appealing accompaniments for mealtime variety

 Sweet Endings **124**
 Fresh, homemade desserts for the perfect finish

Family Fare **151**

 Everyday Favorites **152**
 Fast, family-pleasing recipes for every meal

 Kids in the Kitchen **190**
 Easy, hands-on recipes for aspiring young chefs

Index **220**

154

26

212

What Will You Cook Up Next?

THERE'S MORE TO THE **CROCK-POT**® SLOW COOKER THAN CONVENIENCE. IT'S THE MOST VERSATILE APPLIANCE YOU CAN HAVE IN YOUR KITCHEN!

Slow cooking has definitely evolved over the past decade. Just ask the modern, multi-tasking cooks who have come to depend on their Rival® **CROCK-POT**® Slow Cookers. They've discovered even bigger benefits of slow cooking, above and beyond its obvious convenience. What are those benefits? Versatility and variety.

No other single appliance in the kitchen can match the range of the resourceful **CROCK-POT**® Slow Cooker. It's not only indispensable for putting home-cooked family meals on the table, but also incredibly adept at entertaining and at jazzing up your repertoire. Most impressive of all, however, is the way the **CROCK-POT**® Slow Cooker adapts to your needs—whatever they might be on any given day:

Having a party?
Slow cooking and easy entertaining go hand-in-hand. The **CROCK-POT**® Slow Cooker is a culinary wizard, able to create elegant party fare and ethnic specialties with minimal

Using Your Slow Cooker Year-Round

Regardless of what season it is outside, with a versatile **CROCK-POT**® Slow Cooker in your kitchen, it's always "simmertime"! Fuss-free and climate-friendly for the cook, slow cooking is the perfect way to prepare all your seasonal favorites. This cookbook features lots of great slow cooker recipes to enjoy year-round. Here are just a few:

SPRING
  Asparagus and Cheese
  Bananas Foster
  Coconut Rice Pudding
  Creamy Curried Spinach
  Mediterranean Chicken
  Wild Rice with Fruit & Nuts

SUMMER
  Caponata
  Cioppino
  Corn on the Cob with Garlic Butter
  Roasted Tomato-Basil Soup
  Scalloped Tomatoes & Corn
  Strawberry Rhubarb Crisp

FALL
  Baked Ginger Apples
  Fall-Apart Pork Roast
  German-Style Bratwurst
  Herbed Fall Vegetables
  Orange-Spiced Sweet Potatoes
  Pumpkin-Cranberry Custard

WINTER
  Cran-Cherry Bread Pudding
  Chipotle Chicken Casserole
  Honey Whole-Grain Bread
  Red Hot Applesauce
  "Wake Up to Health" Cereal
  Winter Squash and Apples

So, if you were planning to stash your **CROCK-POT**® Slow Cooker in the cupboard when the weather warms up, think again. With creative, delicious recipes like these, you'll never put your slow cooker away.

effort and maximum results. Plus, using your slow cooker frees up the stovetop and oven when you're cooking for a crowd. It's also a great food warmer for buffets.

Stuck in a rut?

Slow cooking offers unlimited possibilities. The **CROCK-POT**® Slow Cooker ventures easily beyond the main dish, turning out spectacular side dishes, awesome appetizers, and delectable desserts.

Pressed for time?

Slow cooking requires minimal attention: no stirring, no watching, no fussing. Simply prepare the ingredients, turn on your **CROCK-POT**® Slow Cooker, and go take care of something else on your to-do list.

What Will You Cook Up Next? | **5**

Into energy conservation?

Slow cooking really puts the lid on energy use. On the LOW setting, your **CROCK-POT**® Slow Cooker uses only the equivalent power of a 75-watt light bulb.

Busy life?

The **CROCK-POT**® Slow Cooker does the cooking while you're at work or spending quality time with family and friends. And, it's perfectly safe to use while you're away from home.

So, if you've only been using your versatile **CROCK-POT**® Slow Cooker to simmer up traditional soups, stews, chilis, and roasts, it's time to expand your repertoire.

Crock-Pot® *Slow Cooker Recipes for All Occasions* is the perfect place to start. It's creative—chock-full of new ideas, not just variations on the same old standbys. It's unique—with a wider variety of recipes to meet any contemporary cooking challenge. And, it's just what you need to make the most of your **CROCK-POT**® Slow Cooker.

With the **CROCK-POT**® Slow Cooker in your kitchen and *Crock-Pot*® *Slow Cooker Recipes for All Occasions* on the bookshelf, imagine what you'll cook up next!

Concerned about nutrition?

Preparing meals in your **CROCK-POT**® Slow Cooker makes it easier to use more fresh, wholesome ingredients. You can decrease your reliance on prepared mixes or boxed convenience foods and still save time. Plus, it's ideal for creating tender fare from leaner cuts of meat.

Less-than-confident in the kitchen?

Slow cooking is practically foolproof. It's the closest thing to cooking without cooking at all. Cooking in your **CROCK-POT**® Slow Cooker is simple to master and delivers mouth-watering results every time.

Special Recipes for Special Occasions

Your **CROCK-POT**® Slow Cooker isn't just for worry-free weeknights or on-the-go weekends anymore! It also has what it takes to create an impressive variety of elegant fare to share. So put on your party hat! Check out the "Impress Your Guests" chapter to find these inviting and exciting slow cooker recipes.

Holiday Celebration
Turkey with Pecan-Cherry Stuffing
Cran-Orange Acorn Squash
Cran-Cherry Bread Pudding
Chai Tea

Dinner Party
Fall-Apart Pork Roast
Risotto-Style Peppered Rice
Herbed Fall Vegetables
Spicy Fruit Dessert

Ladies' Luncheon
Roasted Tomato-Basil Soup
Stuffed Chicken Breasts
Scalloped Tomatoes and Corn
Poached Pears with Raspberry Sauce

Weekend Brunch
Breakfast Bake
Deluxe Potato Casserole
Chocolate Chip Lemon Loaf
Breakfast Berry Pudding

Appetizer Party
Pizza Fondue
Maple-Glazed Meatballs
Hot Broccoli Cheese Dip
Spicy Sweet & Sour Mini-Franks

Slow Cooking 101

This fast guide to slow cooking will enhance your experience and your results. Additional helpful tips can be found throughout the chapters.

STIRRING

Due to the nature of a slow cooker, there is no need to stir the food unless it specifically says to in your recipe. In fact, taking the lid off to stir food causes the slow cooker to lose a significant amount of heat, extending the cooking time required. Therefore, it is best not to remove the lid for stirring.

COOKING TEMPERATURES AND FOOD SAFETY

Cooking meats in your **CROCK-POT**® Slow Cooker is perfectly safe. According to the U.S. Department of Agriculture, bacteria in food is killed at a temperature of 165°F. Meats cooked in the **CROCK-POT**® Slow Cooker reach an internal temperature in excess of 170°F for beef and as high as 209°F for poultry. It is important to follow the recommended cooking times and to keep the cover on your slow cooker during the cooking process.

If your food isn't done after 8 hours when the recipe calls for 8 to 10 hours, this could be due to voltage variations, which are commonplace everywhere; to altitude; or even to extreme humidity. Slight fluctuations in power do not have a noticeable effect on most appliances; however, they can slightly alter the cooking times. Allow plenty of time, and remember: It is practically impossible to overcook in a slow cooker. You will learn through experience whether to decrease or increase cooking times.

REMOVABLE STONEWARE

The removable stoneware in your **CROCK-POT**® Slow Cooker makes cleaning easy. Here are some tips on the use and care of your stoneware:

• Your **CROCK-POT**® Slow Cooker makes a great server for hot beverages, appetizers, or dips. Keep it on the WARM setting to maintain the proper serving temperature.

• Because all **CROCK-POT**®
Slow Cookers have wrap-around heat,
there is no direct heat at the bottom. For best
results, always fill the stoneware at least half full to conform to
recommended times. Small quantities can still be cooked, but cooking
times will be affected.

BROWNING MEAT

Meat cooked in the **CROCK-POT**® Slow Cooker will not brown as it would if it were cooked in a skillet or oven at high temperatures. For some recipes, it is not necessary to brown meat before slow cooking. If you prefer the flavor and look of browned meat, however, simply brown the meat in a large skillet with nonstick cooking spray before placing it in the stoneware and following the recipe as written.

ADDING INGREDIENTS AT THE END OF THE COOKING TIME

Certain ingredients tend to break down during extended cooking. When possible, add these ingredients toward the end of the cooking time:

● Milk, cream, and sour cream: Add during the last 15 minutes of cooking time.

● Seafood: Add in the last 3 to 15 minutes, depending on the thickness and quantity. Gently stir periodically to ensure even cooking.

COOKING FOR LARGER QUANTITY YIELDS

Follow these guidelines when preparing recipes in a larger unit, such as a 5-, 6-, or 7-quart **CROCK-POT**® Slow Cooker:

● Roasted meats, chicken, and turkey quantities may be doubled or tripled, but seasonings should be adjusted by no more than half. Flavorful seasonings, such as garlic and chili powder, intensify during long, slow cooking. Add just 25 to 50 percent more spices, as needed to balance flavors.
● When preparing a soup or a stew, you may double all ingredients *except* seasonings (see above), dried herbs, liquids, and thickeners. Increase liquid volume by no more than half, or as needed. The **CROCK-POT**® Slow Cooker lid collects steam, which condenses to keep foods moist and to maintain liquid volume. Do not double thickeners, such as cornstarch, at the beginning. You may always add more thickener later if needed.

● When preparing dishes with beef or pork in a larger unit, such as a 5-, 6-, or 7-quart **CROCK-POT**® Slow Cooker, browning the meat in a skillet before adding it to the stoneware yields the best results; the meat will cook more evenly.

● When preparing baked goods, it is best not to double or triple the recipe. Simply prepare the original recipe as many times as needed to serve more people.

Easy Entertaining

Your **CROCK-POT**® Slow Cooker is the secret to entertaining with ease. Imagine all the ways it can serve as your kitchen and catering assistant:

- Prepare parts of the menu ahead of time, so you have energy to enjoy your guests.

- Simmer a sweet treat during dinner, so you can delight your guests with an impressive and inviting warm dessert.

- Gather your guests together and make the festivities more interactive, since slow cooking requires no supervision.

- Create an authentic, slow-simmered ethnic dish without taking expensive cooking classes.

There's almost no end to the ways your **CROCK-POT**® Slow Cooker can help you rise to any occasion—especially with recipes like these that are easy, yet deliver impressive results.

Impress Your Guests

FABULOUS FARE FOR ALL KINDS OF ENTERTAINING OCCASIONS

Spicy Fruit Dessert

MAKES 4 TO 6 SERVINGS

PREP TIME: 10 TO 15 MINUTES

COOK TIME: 4 TO 6 HOURS (LOW) ■ 2 TO 3 HOURS (HIGH)

¼ cup orange marmalade
¼ teaspoon pumpkin pie spice
1 can (6 ounces) frozen orange juice concentrate
2 cups canned pears, drained and diced
2 cups carambola (star fruit), sliced and seeds removed

1. Combine marmalade, pumpkin pie spice, orange juice concentrate, pears and carambola in the **CROCK-POT**® Slow Cooker.

2. Cover; cook on LOW for 4 to 6 hours or on HIGH for 2 to 3 hours or until done. Serve warm over pound cake or ice cream.

Fall-Apart Pork Roast

MAKES 6 SERVINGS

PREP TIME: 10 TO 15 MINUTES

COOK TIME: 7 TO 8 HOURS (LOW) ■ 3 TO 4 HOURS (HIGH)

⅔	cup whole almonds
⅔	cup raisins
3	tablespoons vegetable oil, divided
½	cup chopped onion
4	cloves garlic, chopped
2¾	pounds lean boneless pork shoulder roast, well trimmed
1	can (14½ ounces) diced fire-roasted tomatoes or diced tomatoes, undrained
1	cup cubed bread, any variety
½	cup chicken broth
2	ounces Mexican chocolate, chopped
2	tablespoons chipotle peppers in adobo sauce, chopped
1	teaspoon salt
	Fresh cilantro, coarsely chopped (optional)

1. Heat large skillet over medium-high heat. Add almonds and toast for 3 to 4 minutes, stirring frequently, until fragrant. Add raisins. Cook for 1 to 2 minutes longer, stirring constantly, until raisins begin to plump. Place half of almond mixture in large mixing bowl. Reserve remaining half for garnish.

2. In same skillet, heat 1 tablespoon oil. Add onion and garlic. Cook for 2 to 3 minutes, stirring constantly, until softened. Add to almond mixture; set aside.

3. Heat remaining oil in same skillet. Add pork roast and brown on all sides, about 5 to 7 minutes. Place pork roast in the **CROCK-POT**® Slow Cooker.

4. Combine tomatoes with juice, bread, broth, chocolate, chipotle peppers and salt with the almond mixture. Purée mixture in blender, in 2 or 3 batches, until smooth. Pour purée over pork roast in slow cooker.

5. Cover; cook on LOW for 7 to 8 hours or on HIGH for 3 to 4 hours or until pork is done. Remove pork roast from slow cooker. Whisk sauce in bottom of slow cooker and spoon over pork roast. Garnish with reserved almond mixture and chopped cilantro, if desired.

Risotto-Style Peppered Rice

MAKES 4 TO 6 SERVINGS

PREP TIME: 10 TO 15 MINUTES

COOK TIME: 4 TO 5 HOURS (LOW)

- **1** cup uncooked converted long grain rice
- **1** medium green pepper, chopped
- **1** medium red pepper, chopped
- **1** cup chopped onion
- **½** teaspoon ground turmeric
- **⅛** teaspoon ground red pepper (optional)
- **1** can (14½ ounces) fat-free chicken broth
- **4** ounces Monterey Jack cheese with jalapeño peppers, cubed
- **½** cup milk
- **¼** cup (½ stick) butter, cubed
- **1** teaspoon salt

1. Place rice, peppers, onion, turmeric and ground red pepper, if desired, in the **CROCK-POT**® Slow Cooker. Stir in broth.

2. Cover; cook on LOW for 4 to 5 hours or until rice is done. Stir in cheese, milk, butter and salt; fluff rice with fork. Cover; cook on LOW for 5 minutes or until cheese melts.

Herbed Fall Vegetables

MAKES 6 SERVINGS

PREP TIME: 10 MINUTES

COOK TIME: 4½ HOURS (LOW) ■ 3 HOURS (HIGH)

- 2 medium Yukon gold potatoes, peeled and cut into ½-inch dice
- 2 medium sweet potatoes, peeled and cut into ½-inch dice
- 3 parsnips, peeled and cut into ½-inch dice
- 1 medium head of fennel, sliced and cut into ½-inch dice
- ½ to ¾ cup chopped fresh herbs, such as tarragon, parsley, sage or thyme
- 4 tablespoons butter, cut into small pieces
- 1 cup chicken broth
- 1 tablespoon Dijon mustard
- 1 tablespoon salt
  Freshly ground black pepper to taste

1. Combine potatoes, parsnips, fennel, herbs and butter in the **CROCK-POT**® Slow Cooker.

2. Whisk together broth, mustard, salt and pepper in small bowl. Pour mixture over vegetables.

3. Cook on LOW for 4½ hours or on HIGH for 3 hours until vegetables are tender, stirring occasionally to ensure even cooking.

Breakfast Bake

MAKES 6 TO 8 SERVINGS

PREP TIME: 10 MINUTES

COOK TIME: 3 TO 3½ HOURS (LOW) ■ 2 TO 2½ HOURS (HIGH)

3   to 4 cups diced crusty bread (¾- to 1-inch dice)
½   pound bacon, cut into ½-inch dice
2   cups sliced mushrooms
2   cups torn fresh spinach
8   eggs
½   cup milk
¾   cup roasted red peppers, drained and chopped
1   cup shredded cheese, such as Cheddar or Monterey Jack
    Salt and black pepper to taste

1. Grease the inside of the **CROCK-POT**® Slow Cooker stoneware with nonstick cooking spray. Pour bread into bottom of prepared stoneware.

2. Heat skillet on medium heat. Cook bacon until crispy. Remove all but 1 tablespoon of drippings. Add mushrooms and spinach and toss to coat. Cook for 1 to 2 minutes or until spinach wilts.

3. Beat eggs and milk in medium bowl. Stir in red peppers, cheese, salt and black pepper. Pour into slow cooker.

4. Cover; cook on LOW for 3 to 3½ hours or on HIGH for 2 to 2½ hours, until eggs are firm but still moist. Adjust seasonings.

Breakfast Berry Bread Pudding

MAKES 10 TO 12 SERVINGS

PREP TIME: 10 MINUTES

COOK TIME: 4 TO 4½ HOURS (LOW) ■ 3 HOURS (HIGH)

6	cups bread, preferably dense peasant-style or sourdough, cut into ¾- to 1-inch cubes
½	cup slivered almonds, toasted
1	cup raisins
6	large eggs, beaten
1¾	cup milk (1% or greater)
1	teaspoon vanilla extract
1½	cups brown sugar (increase to 2 cups if making bread pudding for dessert)
1½	teaspoons cinnamon
3	cups sliced fresh strawberries
2	cups fresh blueberries
	Fresh mint leaves (optional)

1. Grease the inside of the **CROCK-POT**® Slow Cooker stoneware with nonstick cooking spray or butter. Place bread, nuts and raisins in prepared stoneware and toss to combine.

2. Whisk together eggs, milk, vanilla, sugar and cinnamon in separate bowl. Pour egg mixture over bread mixture; toss to blend. Cover, cook on LOW for 4 to 4½ hours or on HIGH for 3 hours.

3. Remove stoneware from heating unit and allow bread pudding to cool and set prior to serving. Serve garnished with berries and mint leaves, if desired.

Chocolate Chip Lemon Loaf

MAKES 8 SERVINGS

PREP TIME: 20 TO 30 MINUTES

COOK TIME: 3 TO 4 HOURS (LOW) ■ 1¾ TO 2 HOURS (HIGH)

- ¾ cup granulated sugar
- ½ cup shortening
- 2 eggs, lightly beaten
- 1⅔ cups all-purpose flour
- 1½ teaspoons baking powder
- ¼ teaspoon salt
- ¾ cup milk
- ½ cup chocolate chips
  Grated peel of 1 lemon
  Juice of 1 lemon
- ¼ to ½ cup confectioners' sugar
  Melted chocolate (optional)

1. Preheat a 5-, 6- or 7-quart **CROCK-POT**® Slow Cooker on LOW for about 30 minutes. Grease 2-quart baking dish that will fit inside slow cooker; set aside. Beat granulated sugar and shortening in large bowl until blended. Add eggs, one at a time, mixing well after each addition.

2. Sift together flour, baking powder and salt. Add flour mixture and milk alternately to shortening mixture. Stir in chocolate chips and lemon peel.

3. Spoon batter into prepared dish. Cover with greased foil. Make foil handles (see page 138). Use foil handles to place dish in preheated slow cooker. Cook, with slow cooker lid slightly ajar to allow excess moisture to escape, on LOW for 3 to 4 hours or on HIGH for 1¾ to 2 hours or until edges are golden and knife inserted into center of loaf comes out clean. Remove dish from slow cooker using foil handles; remove foil. Uncover dish; place on wire rack to cool completely.

4. Combine lemon juice and ¼ cup confectioners' sugar in small bowl until smooth. Add more sugar, as needed, to reach desired glaze consistency. Pour glaze over loaf. Drizzle loaf with melted chocolate, if desired.

Deluxe Potato Casserole

MAKES 8 TO 10 SERVINGS

PREP TIME: 10 MINUTES

COOK TIME: 8 TO 10 HOURS (LOW) ■ 5 TO 6 HOURS (HIGH)

1	can (10¾ ounces) condensed cream of chicken soup
1	cup (8 ounces) sour cream
¼	cup chopped onion
¼	cup plus 3 tablespoons melted butter, divided
1	teaspoon salt
2	pounds potatoes, peeled and chopped
2	cups (8 ounces) shredded Cheddar cheese
1½	to 2 cups stuffing mix

1. Combine soup, sour cream, onion, ¼ cup butter and salt in small bowl.

2. Combine potatoes and cheese in the **CROCK-POT**® Slow Cooker. Pour soup mixture over potato mixture; mix well. Sprinkle stuffing mix over potato mixture; drizzle with remaining 3 tablespoons butter.

3. Cover; cook on LOW for 8 to 10 hours or on HIGH for 5 to 6 hours or until potatoes are tender.

HELPFUL HINTS

This is a great brunch dish. Did you know that brunch has become one of America's most popular entertaining options? Since it replaces two meals—breakfast and lunch—a brunch should feature both sweet and savory foods on the menu, plus a variety of entrées, side dishes, beverages and desserts. In addition to the recipes in this chapter, there are other recipes throughout this book that are ideal for brunches:

● Make Chunky Sweet Spiced Apple Butter (page 200) and use it to glaze a baked ham.

● Add Banana Nut Bread (page 162) and Orange Date-Nut Bread (page 166) to the bread basket.

● Try Orange-Spiced Sweet Potatoes (page 106) for a sunny side dish.

Chai Tea

MAKES 8 TO 10 SERVINGS

PREP TIME: 8 MINUTES

COOK TIME: 2 TO 2½ HOURS (HIGH)

- 2 quarts (8 cups) water
- 8 bags black tea
- ¾ cup sugar*
- 16 whole cloves
- 16 whole cardamom seeds, pods removed (optional)
- 5 cinnamon sticks
- 8 slices fresh ginger
- 1 cup milk

*Chai Tea is typically a sweet drink. For less sweetness, reduce sugar to ½ cup.

1. Combine water, tea, sugar, cloves, cardamom, cinnamon and ginger in the **CROCK-POT**® Slow Cooker. Cover; cook on HIGH for 2 to 2½ hours.

2. Strain mixture; discard solids. (May be covered and refrigerated for up to 3 days.)

3. Stir in milk just before serving. Serve warm or chilled.

Turkey with Pecan-Cherry Stuffing

MAKES 8 SERVINGS

PREP TIME: 20 MINUTES

COOK TIME: 5 TO 6 HOURS (LOW)

1   fresh or frozen boneless turkey breast (about 3 to 4 pounds)
2   cups cooked rice
⅓   cup chopped pecans
⅓   cup dried cherries or cranberries
1   teaspoon poultry seasoning
¼   cup peach, apricot or plum preserves
1   teaspoon Worcestershire sauce

1. Thaw turkey breast, if frozen. Remove and discard skin. Cut slices three fourths of the way through turkey at 1-inch intervals.

2. Stir together rice, pecans, cherries and poultry seasoning in large bowl. Stuff rice between slices. If needed, skewer turkey lengthwise to hold together.

3. Place turkey in the **CROCK-POT**® Slow Cooker. Cover; cook on LOW for 5 to 6 hours or until turkey registers 170°F on meat thermometer inserted into thickest part of breast, not touching stuffing.

4. Stir together preserves and Worcestershire sauce. Spoon over turkey. Cover; let stand for 5 minutes. Remove and discard skewer, if used.

Cran-Cherry Bread Pudding

MAKES 12 SERVINGS

PREP TIME: 20 TO 25 MINUTES

COOK TIME: 3½ TO 5½ HOURS (LOW)

- 3 large egg yolks, beaten
- 1½ cups light cream
- ⅓ cup sugar
- ¼ teaspoon kosher salt
- 1½ teaspoons cherry extract
- ⅔ cup sweetened dried cranberries
- ⅔ cup golden raisins
- ½ cup whole candied red cherries, cut in half
- ¾ cup sherry
- 9 cups unseasoned bread stuffing croutons or 18 slices bread, dried in the oven and cut into ½-inch cubes.
- 1 cup white chocolate baking chips
  Whipped cream

1. Combine egg yolks, cream, sugar and salt in medium heavy saucepan. Cook and stir over medium heat until mixture coats a metal spoon. Remove custard from heat; cool at once by setting saucepan in sink of ice water and stirring for 1 to 2 minutes. Stir in cherry extract. Place custard in a large mixing bowl. Cover surface with clear plastic wrap; refrigerate.

2. Combine cranberries, raisins and cherries in small bowl. Heat sherry until warm. Pour over fruits; set aside for 10 minutes.

3. Fold bread cubes and baking chips into custard, until coated. Drain fruits, reserving sherry. Mix fruits with bread cube mixture. Grease 2-quart baking dish that will fit in slow cooker. Pour bread and fruit mixture into prepared dish. Lightly press with back of spoon. Pour reserved sherry over bread mixture; cover dish tightly with foil.

4. Make foil handles (see page 138). Use foil handles to set dish in a 5-, 6- or 7-quart **CROCK-POT**® Slow Cooker. Pour water around dish to depth of 1 inch. Cover; cook on LOW for 3½ to 5½ hours or until pudding springs back when touched. Carefully remove dish from cooker using foil handles; uncover and let stand 10 minutes. Serve warm with whipped cream.

Cran-Orange Acorn Squash

MAKES 6 SERVINGS

PREP TIME: 20 MINUTES

COOK TIME: 2½ HOURS (LOW)

3   small acorn or carnival squash
5   tablespoons instant brown rice
3   tablespoons minced onion
3   tablespoons diced celery
3   tablespoons dried cranberries
      Pinch ground or dried sage leaves
1   teaspoon butter, cut into small pieces
3   tablespoons orange juice
½   cup water

1. Slice off tops of squash and enough of bottoms so squash will sit upright. Scoop out seeds and discard; set squash aside.

2. Combine rice, onion, celery, cranberries and sage in small bowl. Stuff each squash with rice mixture; dot with butter. Pour 1 tablespoon orange juice into each squash over stuffing. Stand squash in the **CROCK-POT**® Slow Cooker. Pour water into bottom of slow cooker.

3. Cover; cook on LOW for 2½ hours or until squash are tender.

Tip: To make slicing off tops and bottoms easier, microwave whole squash on HIGH for 5 minutes.

Scalloped Tomatoes and Corn

MAKES 4 TO 6 SERVINGS

PREP TIME: 7 MINUTES

COOK TIME: 4 TO 6 HOURS (LOW)

- 1 can (15 ounces) cream-style corn
- 1 can (14½ ounces) diced tomatoes, undrained
- ¾ cup saltine cracker crumbs
- 1 egg, lightly beaten
- 2 teaspoons sugar
- ¾ teaspoon pepper

Combine corn, tomatoes with juice, cracker crumbs, egg, sugar and pepper in the **CROCK-POT®** Slow Cooker; mix well. Cover; cook on LOW for 4 to 6 hours or until done.

Stuffed Chicken Breasts

MAKES 6 SERVINGS

PREP TIME: 20 MINUTES

COOK TIME: 5½ TO 6 HOURS (LOW) ■ 4 HOURS (HIGH)

6	boneless, skinless chicken breasts
8	ounces feta cheese, crumbled
3	cups chopped fresh spinach leaves
⅓	cup oil-packed sun-dried tomatoes, drained and chopped
1	teaspoon minced lemon zest
1	teaspoon dried basil, oregano or mint
½	teaspoon garlic powder
	Freshly ground black pepper to taste
1	can (15 ounces) diced tomatoes, undrained
½	cup oil-cured olives*
	Hot cooked polenta

***If using pitted olives, add to slow cooker in the final hour of cooking.**

1. Place 1 chicken breast between plastic wrap. Using the back of skillet or tenderizer mallet, pound breast until about ¼ inch thick. Repeat with each breast.

2. Combine feta, spinach, sun-dried tomatoes, lemon zest, basil, garlic powder and pepper in medium bowl.

3. Lay pounded breasts, smooth side down, on work surface. Place approximately 2 tablespoons feta mixture on wide end of breast. Roll tightly. Repeat with each breast.

4. Place rolled breasts, seam side down, in the **CROCK-POT**® Slow Cooker. Top with diced tomatoes with juice and olives.

5. Cover; cook on LOW for 5½ to 6 hours or on HIGH for 4 hours. Serve with polenta.

Roasted Tomato-Basil Soup

MAKES 6 SERVINGS

PREP TIME: 10 TO 15 MINUTES

COOK TIME: ½ HOUR (450°F OVEN) PLUS 4½ HOURS (HIGH)

2   cans (28 ounces each) peeled whole tomatoes, drained and liquid reserved
2½   tablespoons packed dark brown sugar
1   medium onion, finely chopped
3   cups chicken broth
3   tablespoons tomato paste
¼   teaspoon ground allspice
1   can (5 ounces) evaporated milk
¼   cup shredded fresh basil
    Salt and pepper

1. *Preheat oven to 450°F.* Line baking sheet with foil; spray with nonstick cooking spray. Arrange tomatoes on foil in single layer. Sprinkle with brown sugar and top with onion. Bake for about 30 minutes or until tomatoes look dry and light brown. Let tomatoes cool slightly; finely chop.

2. Place tomato mixture, 3 cups reserved liquid from tomatoes, broth, tomato paste and allspice in the **CROCK-POT**® Slow Cooker. Mix well. Cover; cook on HIGH for 4 hours.

3. Add evaporated milk and basil; season with salt and pepper. Cover; cook on HIGH for 30 minutes or until hot.

Poached Pears with Raspberry Sauce

MAKES 4 TO 5 SERVINGS

PREP TIME: 20 MINUTES

COOK TIME: 3½ TO 4 HOURS (LOW)

- **4** cups cran-raspberry juice cocktail
- **2** cups Rhine or Riesling wine
- **¼** cup sugar
- **2** cinnamon sticks, broken into halves
- **4** to 5 firm Bosc or Anjou pears, peeled and cored
- **1** package (10 ounces) frozen raspberries in syrup, thawed
  Fresh berries (optional)

1. Combine juice, wine, sugar and cinnamon in the **CROCK-POT**® Slow Cooker. Immerse pears in liquid. Cover; cook on LOW for 3½ to 4 hours or until pears are tender. Remove pears and discard cinnamon sticks.

2. Process raspberries in food processor or blender until smooth; strain and discard seeds. Spoon raspberry sauce onto serving plates; place pears on top of sauce. Garnish with fresh berries, if desired.

Maple-Glazed Meatballs

MAKES ABOUT 48 MEATBALLS

PREP TIME: 10 MINUTES

COOK TIME: 5 TO 6 HOURS (LOW)

1½ cups ketchup

1 cup maple syrup or maple-flavored syrup

⅓ cup reduced-sodium soy sauce

1 tablespoon quick-cooking tapioca

1½ teaspoons ground allspice

1 teaspoon dry mustard

2 packages (about 16 ounces each) frozen fully-cooked meatballs

1 can (20 ounces) pineapple chunks in juice, drained

1. Combine ketchup, maple syrup, soy sauce, tapioca, allspice and mustard in the **CROCK-POT**® Slow Cooker.

2. Partially thaw and separate meatballs. Carefully stir meatballs and pineapple chunks into ketchup mixture.

3. Cover; cook on LOW for 5 to 6 hours. Stir before serving. Serve with cocktail picks.

Pizza Fondue

MAKES 20 TO 25 APPETIZER SERVINGS

PREP TIME: 15 MINUTES

COOK TIME: 3 TO 4 HOURS (LOW)

½	pound bulk Italian sausage
1	cup chopped onion
2	jars (26 ounces each) meatless pasta sauce
4	ounces thinly sliced ham, finely chopped
1	package (3 ounces) sliced pepperoni, finely chopped
¼	teaspoon crushed red pepper flakes
1	pound mozzarella cheese, cut into ¾-inch cubes
1	loaf Italian or French bread, cut into 1-inch cubes

1. Cook sausage and onion in large skillet until sausage is browned. Drain off fat. Transfer sausage mixture to the **CROCK-POT**® Slow Cooker. Stir in pasta sauce, ham, pepperoni and pepper flakes.

2. Cover; cook on LOW 3 to 4 hours. Serve fondue with cheese cubes and bread cubes.

Spicy Sweet & Sour Mini-Franks

MAKES ABOUT 4 DOZEN

PREP TIME: 8 MINUTES

COOK TIME: 2 TO 3 HOURS (LOW)

- 2 packages (8 ounces each) mini-franks
- ½ cup ketchup or chili sauce
- ½ cup apricot preserves
- 1 teaspoon hot pepper sauce
  Additional hot pepper sauce, if desired

Combine mini-franks, ketchup, preserves and hot pepper sauce in the **CROCK-POT**® Slow Cooker; mix well. Cover; cook on LOW for 2 to 3 hours. Serve warm or at room temperature with additional hot pepper sauce, if desired.

Hot Broccoli Cheese Dip

MAKES ABOUT 6 CUPS

PREP TIME: 10 TO 15 MINUTES

COOK TIME: 30 MINUTES TO 1 HOUR (HIGH) PLUS 2 TO 4 HOURS (LOW)

- ½ cup butter
- 6 stalks celery, sliced
- 2 onions, chopped
- 2 cans (4 ounces each) sliced mushrooms, drained
- ¼ cup plus 2 tablespoons flour
- 2 cans (10¾ ounces each) condensed cream of celery soup
- 5 to 6 ounces garlic cheese, cut into cubes
- 2 packages (10 ounces each) frozen broccoli spears

Melt butter in large skillet. Add celery, onion and mushrooms; sauté until translucent. Stir in flour and cook for 2 to 3 minutes. Place celery mixture in the **CROCK-POT**® Slow Cooker. Stir in soup, cheese and broccoli. Cover; cook on HIGH, stirring every 15 minutes, until cheese is melted. ***Turn slow cooker to LOW.*** Cover; cook for 2 to 4 hours or until ready to serve.

Wild Mushroom Beef Stew

MAKES 5 SERVINGS

COOK TIME: 10 TO 12 HOURS (LOW) ■ 4 HOURS (HIGH)

1½	to 2 pounds beef stew meat, cut into 1-inch cubes
2	tablespoons all-purpose flour
½	teaspoon salt
½	teaspoon black pepper
1½	cups beef broth
1	teaspoon Worcestershire sauce
1	clove garlic, minced
1	bay leaf
1	teaspoon paprika
4	shiitake mushrooms, sliced
2	medium carrots, sliced
2	medium potatoes, diced
1	small white onion, chopped
1	rib celery, sliced

1. Put the beef in the **CROCK-POT**® Slow Cooker. Mix together the flour, salt and pepper and sprinkle over the meat; stir to coat each piece of meat with flour. Add the remaining ingredients and stir to mix well.

2. Cover; cook on LOW for 10 to 12 hours or on HIGH for 4 to 6 hours. Stir stew before serving.

Note: This classic beef stew is given a twist with the addition of flavorful shiitake mushrooms. If shiitake mushrooms are unavailable in your local grocery store, you can substitute other mushrooms of your choice. For extra punch, add a few dried porcini mushrooms to the stew.

Tip: You may double the amount of meat, mushrooms, carrots, potatoes, onion and celery for the 5-, 6- or 7-quart **CROCK-POT**® Slow Cooker.

Pork Loin with Sherry and Red Onions

MAKES 8 SERVINGS

PREP TIME: 15 MINUTES

COOK TIME: 8 TO 10 HOURS (LOW) ■ 5 TO 6 HOURS (HIGH)

- 3 large red onions, thinly sliced
- 1 cup pearl onions, blanched and peeled
- 2 tablespoons unsalted butter or margarine
- 2½ pounds boneless pork loin, tied
- ½ teaspoon salt
- ½ teaspoon freshly ground black pepper
- ½ cup cooking sherry
- 2 tablespoons Italian parsley, chopped
- 1½ tablespoons cornstarch
- 2 tablespoons water

1. Cook the red onions and pearl onions in the butter in a medium skillet until soft.

2. Rub the pork loin with salt and pepper and place in the **CROCK-POT**® Slow Cooker. Add the cooked onions, sherry and parsley. Cover; cook on LOW for 8 to 10 hours or on HIGH for 5 to 6 hours.

3. Remove the pork loin from the stoneware; let stand 15 minutes before slicing.

4. Combine the cornstarch and water and add to the juice in the stoneware to thicken the sauce. Serve the pork loin with the onions and sherry sauce.

Note: The mild flavor of pork is awakened by this rich, delectable sauce.

Tip: If using the 5-, 6- or 7-quart **CROCK-POT**® Slow Cooker, double all ingredients, except for the sherry, cornstarch and water.

Cajun Chicken and Shrimp Creole

MAKES 6 SERVINGS

PREP TIME: 12 TO 15 MINUTES

COOK TIME: 8 TO 10 HOURS (LOW) ■ 4 TO 5 HOURS (HIGH)

1	pound skinless chicken thighs
1	red bell pepper, chopped
1	large onion, chopped
1	rib celery, diced
1	can (15 ounces) stewed tomatoes, undrained and chopped
1	clove garlic, minced
1	tablespoon sugar
1	teaspoon paprika
1	teaspoon Cajun seasoning
1	teaspoon salt
1	teaspoon freshly ground black pepper
1	pound shelled shrimp, deveined and cleaned
1	tablespoon fresh lemon juice
	Louisiana-style hot sauce to taste
1	cup prepared quick-cooking rice

1. Place the chicken thighs in the **CROCK-POT**® Slow Cooker. Add the bell pepper, onion, celery, tomatoes with juice, garlic, sugar, paprika, Cajun seasoning, salt and pepper.

2. Cover; cook on LOW for 8 to 10 hours or on HIGH for 4 to 5 hours.

3. In the last hour of cooking, add the shrimp, lemon juice and hot sauce. Serve over the hot rice.

Note: Enjoy the full flavors of chicken, shrimp and spices in this delicious creole!

Tip: For a 5-, 6- or 7-quart **CROCK-POT**® Slow Cooker, double all ingredients.

Fresh Herbed Turkey Breast

MAKES 8 SERVINGS

PREP TIME: 5 MINUTES

COOK TIME: 8 TO 10 HOURS (LOW) ■ 4 TO 5 HOURS (HIGH)

2	tablespoons butter, softened
¼	cup fresh sage leaves, minced
¼	cup fresh tarragon leaves, minced
1	clove garlic, minced
1	teaspoon black pepper
½	teaspoon salt
1	(4-pound) split turkey breast
1½	tablespoons cornstarch

1. Mix together the butter, sage, tarragon, garlic, pepper and salt. Rub the butter mixture all over the turkey breast.

2. Place the turkey breast in the **CROCK·POT**® Slow Cooker. Cover; cook on LOW for 8 to 10 hours or on HIGH for 4 to 5 hours or until turkey is no longer pink in the center.

3. Remove the turkey breast from the stoneware. Turn the slow cooker to HIGH; slowly whisk in the cornstarch to thicken the juices. When the sauce is thick and smooth, pour over the turkey breast. Slice to serve.

Note: Fresh herbs enliven this simple, excellent main dish.

Tip: For 5-, 6- or 7-quart **CROCK·POT**® Slow Cooker, double all ingredients.

Country Sausage and Bean Soup

MAKES 9 SERVINGS

PREP TIME: 5 MINUTES

COOK TIME: 8 HOURS (LOW) ■ 4 HOURS PLUS 15 MINUTES (HIGH)

2	cans (14 ounces each) reduced-sodium chicken broth
1½	cups hot water
1	cup dried black beans, sorted and rinsed
1	cup chopped yellow onion
2	bay leaves
1	teaspoon sugar substitute
⅛	teaspoon cayenne pepper
	Cooking spray
6	ounces reduced-fat country pork sausage
1	cup chopped tomato
1	tablespoon Worcestershire sauce
2	teaspoons extra-virgin olive oil
1	tablespoon chili powder
1½	teaspoons ground cumin
½	teaspoon salt
¼	cup chopped cilantro leaves

1. In 3½- to 4-quart **CROCK-POT**® Slow Cooker, combine broth, water, beans, onion, bay leaves, sugar substitute and cayenne. Cover; cook on LOW for 8 hours or on HIGH for 4 hours.

2. Place 10-inch nonstick skillet over medium-high heat until hot. Coat skillet with cooking spray; add sausage and cook until beginning to brown, breaking up large pieces while cooking.

3. Add sausage to bean mixture in slow cooker with remaining ingredients, except cilantro. Cover and cook on HIGH 15 minutes to blend flavors. Add cilantro and serve.

Barley Beef Stroganoff

MAKES 4 SERVINGS

PREP TIME: 10 MINUTES

COOK TIME: 6 TO 7 HOURS (LOW) PLUS 10 TO 15 MINUTES (HIGH)

⅔	cup pearl barley (not quick-cooking)
2½	cups fat-free, low-sodium vegetable broth or water
1	package (6 ounces) sliced mushrooms
½	teaspoon dried marjoram
½	pound very lean ground beef
½	cup chopped celery
½	cup minced green onion
¼	cup fat-free half-and-half
	Minced fresh parsley (optional)

1. Place barley, broth, mushrooms and marjoram in **CROCK-POT**® Slow Cooker on LOW. Cover and cook for 6 to 7 hours.

2. In large nonstick skillet over medium heat, cook and stir ground beef until browned and crumbly, about 7 minutes. Drain away fat. Add celery and onion; cook and stir 3 minutes. Stir beef mixture into slow cooker with half-and-half. Cover and cook on HIGH for 10 to 15 minutes, until beef is hot and vegetables are tender.

3. Garnish with minced fresh parsley, if desired.

Herbed Artichoke Chicken

MAKES 6 SERVINGS

COOK TIME: 6 TO 8 HOURS (LOW) ■ 3½ TO 4 HOURS (HIGH)

1½	pounds boneless, skinless chicken breasts
1	can (14 ounces) tomatoes, drained and diced
1	can (14 ounces) artichoke hearts in water, drained
1	small onion, chopped
½	cup kalamata olives, pitted and sliced
1	cup fat-free chicken broth
¼	cup dry white wine
3	tablespoons quick-cooking tapioca
2	teaspoons curry powder
1	tablespoon chopped fresh Italian parsley
1	teaspoon dried sweet basil
1	teaspoon dried thyme leaves
½	teaspoon salt
½	teaspoon freshly ground black pepper

1. Combine chicken, tomatoes, artichokes, onion, olives, broth, wine, tapioca, curry powder, parsley, basil, thyme, salt and pepper in the **CROCK-POT**® Slow Cooker. Mix thoroughly.

2. Cover; cook on LOW for 6 to 8 hours or on HIGH for 3½ to 4 hours or until chicken is no longer pink in center.

Note: Inviting flavors of tomato, artichokes, Greek olives and herbs imbue the chicken and tease the appetite!

Tip: For a 5-, 6- or 7-quart **CROCK-POT**® Slow Cooker, double all ingredients, except for the chicken broth and white wine. Increase the chicken broth and white wine by one half.

World-Class Cuisine

FESTIVE RECIPES FROM THE MOST POPULAR CUISINES AROUND THE WORLD

Thai Chicken

MAKES 6 SERVINGS

PREP TIME: 10 TO 15 MINUTES

COOK TIME: 8 TO 9 HOURS (LOW) ■ 3 TO 4 HOURS (HIGH)

2½	pounds chicken pieces
1	cup hot salsa
¼	cup peanut butter
2	tablespoons lime juice
1	tablespoon soy sauce
1	teaspoon minced fresh ginger
½	cup peanuts, chopped
2	tablespoons chopped fresh cilantro

1. Place chicken in the **CROCK-POT**® Slow Cooker. Mix together salsa, peanut butter, lime juice, soy sauce and ginger; pour over chicken.

2. Cover; cook on LOW for 8 to 9 hours or on HIGH for 3 to 4 hours or until done.

3. To serve, pour sauce over chicken; sprinkle with peanuts and cilantro.

Best Asian-Style Ribs

MAKES 6 TO 8 SERVINGS

PREP TIME: 10 TO 15 MINUTES

COOK TIME: 6 TO 7 HOURS (LOW) ■ 3 TO 3½ HOURS (HIGH)

2 full racks baby back pork ribs, split into 3 sections each
6 ounces hoisin sauce
2 tablespoons minced fresh ginger
½ cup maraschino cherries
½ cup rice wine vinegar
   Water to cover
4 scallions, chopped

Combine ribs, hoisin sauce, ginger, cherries, vinegar and water in the **CROCK-POT**® Slow Cooker. Cover; cook on LOW for 6 to 7 hours or on HIGH for 3 to 3½ hours or until pork is done. Sprinkle with scallions before serving.

German-Style Bratwurst

MAKES 6 TO 8 SERVINGS

PREP TIME: 10 TO 15 MINUTES

COOK TIME: 6 TO 8 HOURS (LOW) ■ 3 TO 4 HOURS (HIGH)

4 pounds bratwurst
2 pounds sauerkraut, drained
6 apples, peeled, cored and thinly sliced
1 white onion, thinly sliced
1 teaspoon caraway seed
   Freshly ground black pepper
5 bottles (12 ounces each) any German-style beer

Combine bratwurst, sauerkraut, apples, onion, caraway seed, pepper and beer in the **CROCK-POT**® Slow Cooker. Cover; cook on LOW for 6 to 8 hours or on HIGH for 3 to 4 hours or until done.

BEST ASIAN-STYLE RIB

Carne Rellenos

MAKES 6 SERVINGS

PREP TIME: 20 TO 30 MINUTES

COOK TIME: 6 TO 8 HOURS (LOW) ■ 3 TO 4 HOURS (HIGH)

1   can (4 ounces) whole green chilies, drained
4   ounces cream cheese, softened
1   flank steak, about 2 pounds
1½ cups salsa verde

1. Slit whole chilies open on one side with sharp knife; stuff with cream cheese.

2. Open steak flat on sheet of waxed paper; score steak and turn over. Lay stuffed chilies across unscored side of steak. Roll up and tie with kitchen string.

3. Place steak in the **CROCK-POT**® Slow Cooker; pour in salsa. Cover; cook on LOW for 6 to 8 hours or on HIGH for 3 to 4 hours or until done.

4. Remove steak and cut into 6 pieces. Serve with sauce.

Cioppino

MAKES 6 SERVINGS

PREP TIME: 20 TO 30 MINUTES

COOK TIME: 10 TO 12½ HOURS (LOW)

1	pound cod, halibut, or any firm-fleshed white fish, cubed
1	cup mushrooms, sliced
2	carrots, sliced
1	onion, chopped
1	green bell pepper, chopped
1	teaspoon minced garlic
1	can (15 ounces) tomato sauce
1	can (14 ounces) beef broth
1	teaspoon salt
½	teaspoon black pepper
½	teaspoon dried oregano
1	can (7 ounces) cooked clams
½	pound cooked shrimp
1	package (6 ounces) cooked crabmeat
	Minced parsley

1. Combine fish pieces, mushrooms, carrots, onion, green pepper, garlic, tomato sauce, broth, salt, black pepper and oregano in the **CROCK-POT**® Slow Cooker. Cover; cook on LOW for 10 to 12 hours.

2. *Turn slow cooker to HIGH.* Add clams, shrimp and crabmeat. Cover; cook for 30 minutes or until seafood is heated through. Garnish with parsley before serving.

Mediterranean Chicken

MAKES 6 SERVINGS

PREP TIME: 15 TO 20 MINUTES

COOK TIME: 8 TO 10 HOURS (LOW) ■ 4 TO 5 HOURS (HIGH)

1	tablespoon olive oil
2	pounds skinless chicken breasts
	Juice of 2 lemons
2	cinnamon sticks
6	teaspoons minced garlic
1	can (28 ounces) diced tomatoes, undrained
1	bay leaf
½	teaspoon pepper
½	cup sherry
2	onions, chopped
1	pound cooked broad noodles
½	cup feta cheese

1. Heat oil in large skillet. Add the chicken and lightly brown.

2. Combine lemon juice, cinnamon, garlic, tomatoes with juice, bay leaf, pepper, sherry and onions in the **CROCK-POT**® Slow Cooker. Add chicken. Cover; cook on LOW for 8 to 10 hours or on HIGH for 4 to 5 hours or until done.

3. Discard cinnamon sticks and bay leaf. Serve chicken and sauce over cooked noodles. Sprinkle with cheese just before serving.

Moroccan Chicken Tagine

MAKES 4 TO 6 SERVINGS

PREP TIME: 30 TO 45 MINUTES

COOK TIME: 4 TO 5 HOURS (LOW) ■ 15 MINUTES (HIGH)

- 3 pounds chicken pieces, skin removed
- 2 cups chicken broth
- 1 can (14½ ounces) diced tomatoes, undrained
- 2 onions, chopped
- 1 cup dried apricots, chopped
- 4 cloves garlic, minced
- 2 teaspoons ground cumin
- 1 teaspoon cinnamon
- 1 teaspoon ground ginger
- ½ teaspoon ground coriander
- ½ teaspoon ground red pepper
- 6 sprigs fresh cilantro
- 1 tablespoon cornstarch
- 1 tablespoon water
- 1 can (15 ounces) garbanzo beans, rinsed and drained
- 2 tablespoons chopped fresh cilantro
- ¼ cup slivered almonds, toasted*
  Hot cooked couscous or rice

*To toast almonds, spread in single layer on baking sheet. Bake in preheated 350°F oven for 8 to 10 minutes or until golden brown, stirring frequently.

1. Place chicken in the **CROCK-POT**® Slow Cooker. Combine broth, tomatoes with juice, onions, apricots, garlic, cumin, cinnamon, ginger, coriander, red pepper and cilantro in medium bowl; pour over chicken.

2. Cover; cook on LOW for 4 to 5 hours or until chicken is no longer pink in center. Transfer chicken to serving platter; cover to keep warm.

3. Combine cornstarch and water in small bowl; mix until smooth. Stir cornstarch mixture and beans into slow cooker. Cover; cook on HIGH for 15 minutes or until sauce is thickened. Pour sauce over chicken. Sprinkle with cilantro and toasted almonds and serve with couscous.

Caribbean Sweet Potato & Bean Stew

MAKES 4 SERVINGS

PREP TIME: 10 MINUTES

COOK TIME: 5 TO 6 HOURS (LOW)

2   medium sweet potatoes (about 1 pound), peeled and cut into 1-inch cubes
2   cups frozen cut green beans
1   can (15 ounces) black beans, rinsed and drained
1   can (14½ ounces) vegetable broth
1   small onion, sliced
2   teaspoons Caribbean jerk seasoning
½   teaspoon dried thyme
¼   teaspoon salt
¼   teaspoon cinnamon
    Salt and pepper to taste
⅓   cup slivered almonds, toasted*
    Hot pepper sauce (optional)

*To toast almonds, spread in single layer on baking sheet. Bake in preheated 350°F oven for 8 to 10 minutes or until golden brown, stirring frequently.

1. Combine sweet potatoes, green and black beans, broth, onion, jerk seasoning, thyme, salt and cinnamon in the **CROCK-POT**® Slow Cooker.

2. Cover; cook on LOW for 5 to 6 hours or until vegetables are tender.

3. Adjust seasonings. Sprinkle with almonds. Serve with hot pepper sauce, if desired.

Spanish Paella-Style Rice

MAKES 6 SERVINGS

PREP TIME: 10 MINUTES

COOK TIME: 4½ HOURS (LOW)

2	cans (14½ ounces each) chicken broth
1½	cups uncooked converted long grain rice
1	small red bell pepper, diced
⅓	cup dry white wine or water
½	teaspoon powdered saffron or ½ teaspoon ground turmeric
⅛	teaspoon crushed red pepper flakes
½	cup frozen peas, thawed
	Salt

1. Combine broth, rice, pepper, wine, saffron and pepper flakes in the **CROCK-POT**® Slow Cooker; mix well.

2. Cover; cook on LOW for 4 hours or until liquid is absorbed.

3. Stir in peas. Cover; cook for 15 to 30 minutes or until peas are hot. Season with salt.

Note: Paella is a Spanish dish of saffron-flavored rice combined with a variety of meats, seafood and vegetables. Paella is traditionally served in a wide, shallow dish.

Variations: : Add ½ cup cooked chicken, ham, chorizo or seafood when adding peas.

Spanish-Style Couscous

MAKES 4 SERVINGS

PREP TIME: 20 TO 30 MINUTES

COOK TIME: 4 HOURS (LOW)

1	pound lean ground beef
1	can (about **14 ounces**) beef broth
1	small green bell pepper, cut into ½-inch pieces
½	cup pimiento-stuffed green olives, sliced
½	medium onion, chopped
2	cloves garlic, minced
1	teaspoon ground cumin
½	teaspoon dried thyme leaves
1⅓	cups water
1	cup uncooked couscous

1. Heat skillet over high heat until hot. Add beef; cook until browned. Pour off fat. Place broth, pepper, olives, onion, garlic, cumin, thyme and beef in the **CROCK-POT**® Slow Cooker.

2. Cover; cook on LOW for 4 hours or until pepper is tender.

3. Bring water to a boil over high heat in small saucepan. Stir in couscous. Cover; remove from heat. Let stand 5 minutes; fluff with fork. Spoon couscous onto plates; top with beef mixture.

Polenta-Style Corn Casserole

MAKES 6 SERVINGS

PREP TIME: 10 TO 15 MINUTES

COOK TIME: 4 TO 5½ HOURS (LOW) ■ 2 TO 3½ HOURS (HIGH)

1   can (14½ ounces) chicken broth
½   cup cornmeal
1   can (7 ounces) corn, drained
1   can (4 ounces) green chilies, drained
¼   cup diced red bell pepper
½   teaspoon salt
¼   teaspoon black pepper
1   cup shredded Cheddar cheese

1. Pour chicken broth into the **CROCK-POT**® Slow Cooker. Whisk in cornmeal. Add corn, chilies, red pepper, salt and black pepper. Cover; cook on LOW for 4 to 5 hours or on HIGH for 2 to 3 hours.

2. Stir in cheese. Continue cooking, uncovered, 15 to 30 minutes or until cheese melts.

Serving Suggestion: Divide cooked corn mixture into lightly greased individual ramekins or spread in pie plate; cover and refrigerate. Serve at room temperature or warm in oven or microwave.

Ratatouille with Garbanzo Beans

MAKES 6 TO 8 SERVINGS

PREP TIME: 15 MINUTES

COOK TIME: 7 TO 8 HOURS (LOW) ■ 4½ TO 5 HOURS (HIGH)

- 3 tablespoons olive oil, divided
- 4 cloves garlic, minced
- 1 yellow onion, cut into ½-inch dice
- 4 small Italian eggplant, peeled and chopped into ¾- to 1-inch dice
  Salt and black pepper to taste
- 1 red bell pepper, seeded and cut into ¾- to 1-inch dice
- 1 yellow bell pepper, seeded and cut into ¾- to 1-inch dice
- 1 orange bell pepper, seeded and cut into ¾- to 1-inch dice
- 3 small zucchini, cut into ¾-inch dice
- 1 can (15 to 20 ounces) garbanzo beans, rinsed and drained
- 2 cups crushed tomatoes
- ¼ cup fresh basil leaves
- 2 tablespoons chopped fresh thyme
- ½ to 1 teaspoon crushed red pepper flakes
  Fresh basil leaves for garnish (optional)

1. Heat 1 tablespoon oil in skillet on medium-low. Add garlic and onion and cook for 2 to 3 minutes or until translucent. Add eggplant, season with salt and black pepper, and cook for 1 to 2 minutes. Turn heat to low and cover. Cook until eggplant is tender, 4 to 5 minutes. Transfer to the **CROCK-POT**® Slow Cooker.

2. Add peppers, zucchini and garbanzo beans to slow cooker.

3. Combine tomatoes, basil, thyme, pepper flakes and remaining 2 tablespoons oil in medium bowl. Blend and pour into slow cooker. Stir together all ingredients.

4. Cover; cook on LOW for 7 to 8 hours or on HIGH for 4½ to 5 hours or until vegetables are tender. Adjust seasonings. Garnish with basil, if desired.

Korean BBQ Beef Short Ribs

MAKES 6 SERVINGS

PREP TIME: 10 TO 15 MINUTES

COOK TIME: 7½ TO 8½ HOURS (LOW) ■ 3½ TO 4½ HOURS (HIGH)

4	to 4½ pounds beef short ribs
¼	cup chopped green onions with tops
¼	cup tamari or soy sauce
¼	cup beef broth or water
1	tablespoon brown sugar
2	teaspoons minced fresh ginger
2	teaspoons minced garlic
½	teaspoon pepper
2	teaspoons Asian sesame oil
	Hot cooked rice or linguine pasta
2	teaspoons sesame seeds, toasted

1. Place ribs in the **CROCK-POT**® Slow Cooker. Combine green onions, soy sauce, broth, brown sugar, ginger, garlic and pepper in medium bowl; mix well and pour over ribs. Cover; cook on LOW for 7 to 8 hours or on HIGH for 3 to 4 hours or until ribs are fork tender.

2. Remove ribs from cooking liquid, cool slightly. Trim excess fat. Cut rib meat into bite-sized pieces discarding bones and fat.

3. Let cooking liquid stand 5 minutes to allow fat to rise. Skim off fat.

4. Stir sesame oil into liquid. Return beef to slow cooker. ***Turn slow cooker to LOW, if needed.*** Cover; cook on LOW for 15 to 30 minutes or until mixture is hot.

5. Serve with rice or pasta and garnish with sesame seeds.

Risi Bisi

PREP TIME: 15 MINUTES

COOK TIME: 3 TO 4 HOURS (LOW)

1½   **cups converted long-grain white rice**
¾   **cup chopped onion**
2   **cloves garlic, minced**
2   **cans (about 14 ounces each) reduced-sodium chicken broth**
⅓   **cup water**
¾   **teaspoon Italian seasoning**
½   **teaspoon dried basil leaves**
½   **cup frozen peas, thawed**
¼   **cup grated Parmesan cheese**
¼   **cup toasted pine nuts (optional)**

1. Combine rice, onion and garlic in the **CROCK-POT**® Slow Cooker. Heat broth and water in small saucepan to a boil. Stir boiling liquid, Italian seasoning and basil into rice mixture. Cover; cook on LOW for 2 to 3 hours or until liquid is absorbed.

2. Add peas. Cover; cook 1 hour. Stir in cheese. Spoon rice into serving bowl. Sprinkle with pine nuts, if desired.

Quatro Frioles Con Pollo Cantaro

MAKES 6 SERVINGS

PREP TIME: 15 MINUTES

COOK TIME: 4 TO 5 HOURS (LOW))

- 1   cup ripe pitted black olives, drained
- 1   pound boneless, skinless chicken* breasts, cubed
- 1   can (16 ounces) garbanzo beans, rinsed and drained
- 1   can (16 ounces) Great Northern or navy beans, drained and rinsed
- 1   can (15 ounces) cannellini beans, drained and rinsed
- 1   can (16 ounces) red kidney beans, rinsed and drained
- 1   can (7 ounces) chopped mild green chilies, drained
- 2   cups chicken stock, plus extra as needed
- 2   tablespoons canola or olive oil
- 1   cup minced onions
- 2   teaspoons minced garlic
- 1½ teaspoons ground cumin
     Hot sauce to taste
     Salt and black pepper to taste
- 2   cups crushed corn chips
- 6   ounces Monterey Jack cheese, grated

*Turkey, pork or beef can be substituted for the chicken.

1. Combine olives, chicken, beans, chilies and chicken stock in **CROCK-POT**® slow cooker. Mix well; set aside.

2. Heat oil in large skillet over medium-high heat. Cook onion, garlic and cumin until onions are soft, stirring frequently. Add to chicken mixture. Cover and cook on LOW for 4 to 5 hours. Check liquid about halfway through, adding more hot broth as needed.

3. Add hot sauce, salt and pepper to taste. Serve in warm bowls and garnish with corn chips and cheese.

Chicken Provençal

MAKES 8 SERVINGS

PREP TIME: 15 TO 20 MINUTES

COOK TIME: 7 TO 9 HOURS (LOW) ■ 3 TO 4 HOURS (HIGH)

2   pounds boneless, skinless chicken thighs, each cut into quarters
2   medium red peppers, cut into ¼-inch-thick slices
1   medium yellow pepper, cut into ¼-inch-thick slices
1   onion, thinly sliced
1   (28-ounce) can plum tomatoes, drained
3   cloves garlic, minced
¼   teaspoon salt
¼   teaspoon thyme
¼   teaspoon fennel seeds, crushed
3   strips orange peel
½   cup fresh basil leaves, chopped

1. Place thighs, bell peppers, onion, tomatoes, garlic, salt, thyme, fennel seeds and orange peel in the **CROCK-POT**® Slow Cooker. Mix thoroughly.

2. Cover; cook on LOW for 7 to 9 hours or on HIGH for 3 to 4 hours. Sprinkle with basil before serving.

Note: This Southern French chicken dish contrasts the citrus with the sweet. Serve with a crusty French baguette and seasonal vegetables.

Tip: You may double all the ingredients when using a 5-, 6- or 7-quart **CROCK-POT**® Slow Cooker.

Asian-Spiced Chicken Wings

MAKES 10 TO 16 WINGS

PREP TIME: 25 MINUTES

COOK TIME: 5 TO 6 HOURS (LOW) ■ 2 TO 3 HOURS (HIGH)

3	pounds chicken wings
1	cup packed brown sugar
1	cup soy sauce
½	cup ketchup
2	teaspoons fresh ginger, minced
2	cloves garlic, minced
¼	cup dry sherry
½	cup hoisin sauce
1	tablespoon fresh lime juice
3	tablespoons sesame seeds, toasted
¼	cup green onions, thinly sliced

1. Broil the chicken wings 10 minutes on each side, or until browned. Transfer the chicken wings to the **CROCK-POT**® Slow Cooker. Add the remaining ingredients, except the hoisin sauce, lime juice, sesame seeds and green onions; stir thoroughly. Cover; cook on LOW for 5 to 6 hours or on HIGH for 2 to 3 hours or until the wings are no longer pink, stirring once halfway through the cooking time to baste the wings with sauce.

2. Remove wings from stoneware. Reserve ¼ cup of the juices in the slow cooker and combine with the hoisin sauce and lime juice. Drizzle mixture over the wings.

3. Before serving, sprinkle the wings with the sesame seeds and green onions.

Note: Chicken wings are always crowd pleasers. Garnishing them with toasted sesame seeds and green onions gives these appetizers added crunch and contrasting color.

Tip: For 5-, 6- or 7-quart **CROCK-POT**® Slow Cooker, increase chicken wings to 5 pounds.

Simple Coq au Vin

MAKES 4 SERVINGS

PREP TIME: 10 TO 15 MINUTES

COOK TIME: 8 TO 10 HOURS (LOW) ■ 3 TO 4 HOURS (HIGH)

4	chicken legs
	Salt and black pepper
2	tablespoons olive oil
½	pound mushrooms, sliced
1	onion, sliced into rings
½	cup red wine
½	teaspoon dried basil leaves
½	teaspoon dried thyme leaves
½	teaspoon dried oregano leaves
	Hot cooked rice

1. Sprinkle chicken with salt and pepper. Heat oil in large skillet; brown chicken on both sides. Remove chicken and place in the **CROCK-POT**® Slow Cooker. Sauté mushrooms and onion in same skillet. Add wine; stir and scrape brown bits from bottom of skillet. Add mixture to slow cooker. Sprinkle with basil, thyme and oregano.

2. Cover and cook on LOW for 8 to 10 hours or on HIGH for 3 to 4 hours.

3. Serve chicken and sauce over rice.

Mediterranean Stew

MAKES 6 SERVINGS

PREP TIME: 5 MINUTES

COOK TIME: 8 TO 10 HOURS (LOW)

- 1   medium butternut or acorn squash, peeled and cut into 1-inch cubes
- 2   cups unpeeled eggplant, cut into 1-inch cubes
- 2   cups sliced zucchini
- 1   can (15½ ounces) chickpeas (garbanzo beans), rinsed and drained
- 1   package (10 ounces) frozen cut okra
- 1   can (8 ounces) tomato sauce
- 1   cup chopped onion
- 1   medium tomato, chopped
- 1   medium carrot, thinly sliced
- ½   cup reduced-sodium vegetable broth
- ⅓   cup raisins
- 1   clove garlic, minced
- ½   teaspoon ground cumin
- ½   teaspoon ground turmeric
- ¼   to ½ teaspoon ground red pepper
- ¼   teaspoon ground cinnamon
- ¼   teaspoon paprika
- 6   to 8 cups hot cooked couscous or rice
    Fresh parsley (optional)

1. Combine squash, eggplant, zucchini, chickpeas, okra, tomato sauce, onion, tomato, carrot, broth, raisins, garlic, cumin, turmeric, red pepper, cinnamon and paprika in the **CROCK-POT**® Slow Cooker; mix well.

2. Cover; cook on LOW for 8 to 10 hours or until vegetables are crisp-tender.

3. Serve over couscous. Garnish with parsley, if desired.

Forty-Clove Chicken

MAKES 4 TO 6 SERVINGS

PREP TIME: 10 TO 15 MINUTES

COOK TIME: 6 HOURS (LOW)

1 frying chicken (3 pounds), cut up
Salt and black pepper
1 to 2 tablespoons olive oil
¼ cup dry white wine
2 tablespoons chopped fresh parsley or 2 teaspoons dried
parsley flakes
2 tablespoons dry vermouth
2 teaspoons dried basil leaves
1 teaspoon dried oregano leaves
Pinch red pepper flakes
40 cloves garlic (about 2 heads*), peeled
4 ribs celery, sliced
Juice and peel of 1 lemon
Fresh herbs

*The whole garlic bulb is called a head.

1. Remove skin from chicken. Sprinkle chicken with salt and pepper. Heat oil in large skillet over medium heat. Add chicken; brown on all sides. Remove to platter.

2. Combine wine, parsley, vermouth, basil, oregano and red pepper flakes in large bowl. Add garlic and celery; coat well. Transfer garlic and celery to the **CROCK-POT**® Slow Cooker with slotted spoon. Add chicken to remaining herb mixture; coat well. Place chicken on top of celery mixture in slow cooker. Sprinkle lemon juice and peel over chicken; add remaining herb mixture.

3. Cover; cook on LOW for 6 hours. Sprinkle with fresh herbs before serving.

Slow-Simmered Jambalaya

MAKES 4 TO 6 SERVINGS

PREP TIME: 5 MINUTES

COOK TIME: 8 TO 10 HOURS (LOW)

- 2 cans (14½ ounces each) stewed tomatoes, undrained
- 2 cups diced boiled ham
- 2 medium onions, coarsely chopped
- 1 medium green bell pepper, diced
- 2 ribs celery, sliced
- 1 cup uncooked long-grain converted rice
- 2 tablespoons vegetable oil
- 2 tablespoons ketchup
- 3 cloves garlic, minced
- ½ teaspoon dried thyme leaves
- ½ teaspoon black pepper
- ⅛ teaspoon ground cloves
- 1 pound fresh or frozen uncooked shrimp, peeled and deveined

1. Combine tomatoes with juice, ham, onions, bell pepper, celery, rice, oil, ketchup, garlic, thyme, black pepper and cloves in the **CROCK-POT**® Slow Cooker.

2. Cover; cook on LOW for 8 to 10 hours.

3. One hour before serving, increase heat to HIGH. Stir in uncooked shrimp. Cover; cook until shrimp are pink and tender.

Beef Bourguignonne

MAKES 10 TO 12 SERVINGS

PREP TIME: 10 MINUTES

COOK TIME: 8 TO 9 HOURS (LOW) ■ 2 TO 3 HOURS (HIGH)

1	to 2 boneless beef top sirloin steaks (about 3 pounds)
½	cup all-purpose flour
4	slices bacon, diced
2	medium carrots, diced
8	small red potatoes, unpeeled, cut into quarters
8	to 10 mushrooms, sliced
20	to 24 pearl onions
3	cloves garlic, minced
1	bay leaf
1	teaspoon dried marjoram leaves
½	teaspoon dried thyme leaves
½	teaspoon salt
	Black pepper
2½	cups Burgundy wine or beef broth

1. Cut beef into 1-inch pieces. Coat with flour, shaking off excess; set aside. Cook bacon in large skillet over medium heat until partially cooked. Add beef; brown on all sides. Drain and discard fat.

2. Layer carrots, potatoes, mushrooms, onions, garlic, bay leaf, marjoram, thyme, salt, pepper and beef mixture in the **CROCK-POT**® Slow Cooker. Pour wine over all.

3. Cover; cook on LOW for 8 to 9 hours or on HIGH for 2 to 3 hours until beef is tender. Remove and discard bay leaf before serving.

Slow-Simmered Curried Chicken

MAKES 4 SERVINGS

PREP TIME: 5 MINUTES

COOK TIME: 5 TO 6 HOURS (LOW) PLUS 15 MINUTES (HIGH)

1½	cups chopped onion
1	medium green bell pepper, chopped
1	pound boneless, skinless chicken breasts or thighs, cut into bite-sized pieces
1	cup medium salsa
2	teaspoons grated fresh ginger
½	teaspoon garlic powder
½	teaspoon red pepper flakes
¼	cup chopped fresh cilantro
1	teaspoon sugar
1	teaspoon curry powder
¾	teaspoon salt
	Hot cooked rice

1. Place onion and bell pepper in the **CROCK-POT**® Slow Cooker; top with chicken. Combine salsa, ginger, garlic powder and pepper flakes in small bowl; spoon over chicken.

2. Cover; cook on LOW for 5 to 6 hours, or until chicken is tender.

3. Combine cilantro, sugar, curry powder and salt in small bowl; stir into slow cooker. Cover; cook on HIGH for 15 minutes or until hot. Serve with rice.

Arroz Con Queso

MAKES 8 TO 10 SERVINGS

PREP TIME: 10 TO 15 MINUTES

COOK TIME: 6 TO 9 HOURS (LOW)

1	can (16 ounces) whole tomatoes, mashed
1	can (15 ounces) black beans, rinsed and drained
1½	cups uncooked long grain converted rice
1	onion, chopped
1	cup cottage cheese
1	can (4 ounces) chopped green chilies
2	tablespoons vegetable oil
3	teaspoons minced garlic
2	cups grated Monterey Jack cheese, divided

1. Combine tomatoes, beans, rice, onion, cottage cheese, chilies, oil, garlic and 1 cup Monterey Jack cheese in the **CROCK-POT**® Slow Cooker; mix thoroughly.

2. Cover; cook on LOW for 6 to 9 hours or until liquid is absorbed. Sprinkle with remaining cheese before serving.

Beyond the Entrée

Variety isn't Just the spice of life. It's a key ingredient in the recipe for eating right. For nutritional balance, as well as avoiding boredom, experts suggest we eat lots of different foods. Your versatile **CROCK-POT**® Slow Cooker is like your personal chef, ready to put more variety on the plate—including hearty grains, succulent vegetables, and fruit-based favorites:

- Come home to fresh, perfectly cooked complements for grilled steaks, chops, seafood, or chicken,

- Round out your holiday dinner menu by making slow-cooked side dishes while the roast is in the oven.

- Slow cook some special sides or a yummy dessert to add interest and pizzazz to a meal of leftovers.

With multiple **CROCK-POT**® Slow Cookers in your kitchen, you can multiply the convenience and variety even more. You'll have your cake and rice and beef stew, too—all ready and waiting when you walk in the door!

Spectacular Sides

APPEALING ACCOMPANIMENTS FOR MEALTIME VARIETY

Asparagus and Cheese

MAKES 4 TO 6 SERVINGS

PREP TIME: 10 MINUTES

COOK TIME: 3 TO 3½ HOURS (HIGH)

1½	pounds fresh asparagus, trimmed
2	cups crushed saltine crackers
1	can (10¾ ounces) condensed cream of asparagus soup
1	can (10¾ ounces) condensed cream of chicken soup
⅔	cup slivered almonds
4	ounces American cheese, cut into cubes
1	egg

Combine asparagus, crackers, soups, almonds, cheese and egg in large bowl; stir well. Pour into the **CROCK-POT**® Slow Cooker. Cover; cook on HIGH for 3 to 3½ hours or until done.

Spinach Gorgonzola Corn Bread

MAKES 10 TO 12 SERVINGS

PREP TIME: 8 MINUTES

COOK TIME: 1½ HOURS (HIGH)

- 2 boxes (8½ ounces each) cornbread mix
- 3 eggs
- ½ cup cream
- 1 box (10 ounces) frozen chopped spinach, thawed and drained
- 1 cup gorgonzola cheese crumbles
- 1 teaspoon pepper

Mix cornbread mix, eggs, cream, spinach, cheese and pepper in medium bowl. Grease the inside of the **CROCK-POT**® Slow Cooker stoneware; add batter. Cover; cook on HIGH for 1½ hours or until done.

Note: Cook only on HIGH setting for proper crust and texture.

Creamy Curried Spinach

MAKES 6 TO 8 SERVINGS

PREP TIME: 10 TO 15 MINUTES

COOK TIME: 3 TO 4 HOURS (LOW) ■ 2 HOURS (HIGH)

- 3 packages (10 ounces each) frozen spinach, thawed
- 1 onion, chopped
- 4 teaspoons minced garlic
- 2 tablespoons curry powder
- 2 tablespoons butter, melted
- ¼ cup chicken broth
- ¼ cup heavy cream
- 1 teaspoon lemon juice

Combine spinach, onion, garlic, curry powder, butter and broth in the **CROCK-POT**® Slow Cooker. Cover; cook on LOW for 3 to 4 hours or on HIGH for 2 hours or until done. Stir in cream and lemon juice *30 minutes before end of cooking time*.

SPINACH GORGONZOLA CORN BREAD

Supper Squash Medley

MAKES 8 TO 10 SERVINGS

PREP TIME: 15 TO 20 MINUTES

COOK TIME: 6½ HOURS (LOW)

- 2   butternut squash, peeled, seeded and diced
- 1   can (28 ounces) tomatoes, undrained
- 1   can (15 ounces) corn, drained
- 2   onions, chopped
- 2   teaspoons minced garlic
- 2   green chilies, chopped
- 2   green bell peppers, chopped
- 1   cup chicken broth
- 1   teaspoon salt
- ½   teaspoon black pepper
- 1   can (6 ounces) tomato paste

1. Combine squash, tomatoes with juice, corn, onions, garlic, chilies, green peppers, broth, salt and black pepper in the **CROCK-POT**® Slow Cooker. Cover; cook on LOW for 6 hours.

2. Remove about ½ cup cooking liquid and blend with tomato paste. Stir mixture into slow cooker. Cook 30 minutes or until mixture is slightly thickened and heated through.

Wild Rice and Mushroom Casserole

MAKES 4 TO 6 SERVINGS

PREP TIME: 10 TO 15 MINUTES

COOK TIME: 4 TO 6 HOURS (LOW) ■ 2 TO 3 HOURS (HIGH)

- 2 tablespoons olive oil
- ½ medium red onion, finely diced
- 1 large green bell pepper, finely diced
- 8 ounces button mushrooms, thinly sliced
- 2 cloves garlic, minced
- 1 can (14 ounces) diced tomatoes, drained
- 1 teaspoon dried oregano
- 1 teaspoon paprika
- 2 tablespoons butter
- 2 tablespoons flour
- 1½ cups milk
- 8 ounces Pepper-Jack, Cheddar or Swiss cheese, shredded
- 1 teaspoon salt
- ½ teaspoon freshly ground black pepper
- 2 cups wild rice, cooked according to package instructions

1. Heat oil in large skillet over medium heat. Add onion, green pepper and mushrooms. Sauté 5 to 6 minutes, stirring occasionally, until vegetables soften. Add garlic, tomatoes, oregano and paprika. Continue to sauté until heated through. Remove to large mixing bowl to cool.

2. Melt butter in the same skillet over medium heat; whisk in flour. Cook and stir until smooth and golden, about 4 to 5 minutes. Whisk in milk and bring to a boil. Whisk shredded cheese into boiling milk to produce rich, velvety sauce.

3. Combine cooked wild rice with sautéed vegetables in large mixing bowl. Fold in the cheese sauce and mix gently.

4. Grease the inside of the **CROCK-POT**® Slow Cooker stoneware. Pour the wild rice mixture into the prepared stoneware. Cover; cook on LOW for 4 to 6 hours or on HIGH for 2 to 3 hours or until done.

Caponata

MAKES ABOUT 5 SERVINGS

PREP TIME: 20 TO 25 MINUTES

COOK TIME: 7 TO 8 HOURS (LOW)

1   medium eggplant (about 1 pound), peeled and cut into ½-inch pieces
1   can (14½ ounces) diced Italian plum tomatoes, undrained
1   medium onion, chopped
1   red bell pepper, cut into ½-inch pieces
½   cup medium-hot salsa
¼   cup extra-virgin olive oil
2   tablespoons capers, drained
2   tablespoons balsamic vinegar
3   cloves garlic, minced
1   teaspoon dried oregano
¼   teaspoon salt
⅓   cup packed fresh basil, cut into thin strips
    Toasted sliced Italian or French bread

1. Mix eggplant, tomatoes with juice, onion, pepper, salsa, oil, capers, vinegar, garlic, oregano and salt in the **CROCK-POT**® Slow Cooker.

2. Cover; cook on LOW for 7 to 8 hours or until vegetables are crisp-tender.

3. Stir in basil. Serve at room temperature on toasted bread.

HELPFUL HINTS

When using the **CROCK-POT**® Slow Cooker, fresh herbs are best added during the last 15 minutes of cooking time. This helps them retain flavor and their vibrant color.

One other spice note to remember: When slow cooking, you may want to use *whole* herbs and spices rather than crushed or ground. The flavor and aroma of crushed or ground spices may lessen during the extended cooking time. Be sure to taste and adjust seasonings before serving.

Southwestern Corn and Beans

MAKES 6 SERVINGS

PREP TIME: 15 MINUTES

COOK TIME: 7 TO 8 HOURS (LOW) ■ 2 TO 3 HOURS (HIGH)

- 1 tablespoon olive oil
- 1 large onion, diced
- 1 or 2 jalapeño peppers,* diced
- 1 clove garlic, minced
- 2 cans (15 ounces) light red kidney beans, rinsed and drained
- 1 bag (16 ounces) frozen corn, thawed
- 1 can (14½ ounces) diced tomatoes, undrained
- 1 green bell pepper, cut into 1-inch pieces
- 2 teaspoons medium-hot chili powder
- ¾ teaspoon salt
- ½ teaspoon ground cumin
- ½ teaspoon black pepper
  Sour cream or plain yogurt (optional)
  Sliced black olives (optional)

*Jalapeño peppers can sting and irritate the skin; wear rubber gloves when handling peppers and do not touch eyes. Wash hands after handling.

1. Heat oil in medium skillet over medium heat. Add onion, jalapeño and garlic; cook 5 minutes. Combine onion mixture, kidney beans, corn, tomatoes with juice, green pepper, chili powder, salt, cumin and black pepper in the **CROCK-POT**® Slow Cooker; mix well.

2. Cover; cook on LOW for 7 to 8 hours or on HIGH for 2 to 3 hours or until done.

3. Serve with sour cream and black olives, if desired.

Serving suggestion: For a party, spoon this colorful vegetarian dish into hollowed-out bell peppers or bread bowls.

Orange-Spiced Sweet Potatoes

MAKES 8 SERVINGS

PREP TIME: 10 TO 15 MINUTES

COOK TIME: 4 HOURS (LOW) ■ 2 HOURS (HIGH)

2	pounds sweet potatoes, peeled and diced
½	cup packed dark brown sugar
½	cup butter (1 stick), cut into small pieces
1	teaspoon cinnamon
½	teaspoon ground nutmeg
½	teaspoon grated orange peel
	Juice of 1 medium orange
¼	teaspoon salt
1	teaspoon vanilla
	Chopped toasted pecans (optional)

Place sweet potatoes, brown sugar, butter, cinnamon, nutmeg, orange peel, orange juice, salt and vanilla in the **CROCK-POT**® Slow Cooker. Cover; cook on LOW for 4 hours or on HIGH for 2 hours or until potatoes are tender. Sprinkle with pecans before serving, if desired.

Variation: Mash potatoes; add ¼ cup milk or whipping cream. Sprinkle with a mixture of sugar and cinnamon.

Vegetable Curry

MAKES 6 SERVINGS

PREP TIME: 10 TO 15 MINUTES

COOK TIME: 8 TO 9 HOURS (LOW)

4	potatoes, diced
1	onion, chopped
1	red bell pepper, chopped
2	carrots, diced
2	tomatoes, chopped
1	can (6 ounces) tomato paste
¾	cup water
2	teaspoons cumin seeds
½	teaspoon garlic powder
½	teaspoon salt
3	cups cauliflower
1	package (10 ounces) frozen peas, thawed

Combine potatoes, onions, pepper, carrots and tomatoes in the **CROCK-POT**® Slow Cooker. Stir in tomato paste, water, cumin seeds, garlic powder and salt. Stir and add cauliflower. Cover; cook on LOW for 8 to 9 hours or until done. Stir in peas before serving.

Escalloped Corn

MAKES 6 SERVINGS

PREP TIME: 7 MINUTES

COOK TIME: 3½ TO 4 HOURS (LOW)

2	tablespoons butter
½	cup chopped onion
3	tablespoons all-purpose flour
1	cup milk
4	cups frozen corn, thawed, divided
½	teaspoon salt
½	teaspoon dried thyme leaves
¼	teaspoon black pepper
⅛	teaspoon ground nutmeg
	Fresh thyme (optional)

1. Melt butter in small saucepan over medium heat. Add onion; cook and stir 5 minutes or until tender. Add flour. Cook over medium heat 1 minute, stirring constantly. Stir in milk; bring to a boil. Boil 1 minute or until thickened, stirring constantly.

2. Process 2 cups corn in food processor or blender until coarsely chopped. Combine milk mixture, chopped and whole corn, salt, dried thyme, pepper and nutmeg in **CROCK-POT**® Slow Cooker; mix well.

3. Cover; cook on LOW for 3½ to 4 hours or until mixture is bubbly around edge. Garnish with fresh thyme, if desired.

Variation: Add ½ cup (2 ounces) shredded Cheddar cheese and 2 tablespoons grated Parmesan cheese before serving; stir until melted. Garnish with additional shredded Cheddar cheese.

Scalloped Potatoes and Parsnips

MAKES 4 TO 6 SERVINGS

PREP TIME: 15 TO 20 MINUTES

COOK TIME: 7 HOURS (LOW) ■ 3½ HOURS (HIGH)

- 6 tablespoons unsalted butter
- 3 tablespoons all-purpose flour
- 1¾ cups heavy cream
- 2 teaspoons dry mustard
- 1½ teaspoons salt
- 1 teaspoon dried thyme
- ½ teaspoon pepper
- 2 baking potatoes, peeled, cut in half lengthwise, then cut into ¼-inch slices crosswise
- 2 parsnips, peeled and cut into ¼-inch slices
- 1 onion, chopped
- 2 cups (8 ounces) shredded sharp Cheddar cheese

1. Melt butter in medium saucepan over medium-high heat. Add flour and whisk constantly 3 to 5 minutes. Slowly whisk in cream, mustard, salt, thyme and pepper. Stir until smooth.

2. Place potatoes, parsnips and onion in the **CROCK-POT**® Slow Cooker. Add cream sauce.

3. Cover; cook on LOW for 7 hours or on HIGH for 3½ hours or until potatoes are tender. Stir in cheese. Cover; let stand until cheese melts.

Red Cabbage and Apples

MAKES 4 TO 6 SERVINGS

PREP TIME: 15 TO 20 MINUTES

COOK TIME: 6 HOURS (HIGH)

- 1   small head red cabbage, cored and thinly sliced
- 3   medium apples, peeled and grated
- ¼   cup sugar
- ½   cup red wine vinegar
- 1   teaspoon ground cloves
- 1   cup crisp-cooked and crumbled bacon (optional)

Mix together cabbage, apples, sugar, vinegar and cloves in the **CROCK-POT®** Slow Cooker. Cover; cook on HIGH for 6 hours, stirring after 3 hours. Sprinkle with bacon before serving, if desired.

Corn on the Cob with Garlic Herb Butter

MAKES 4 TO 5 SERVINGS

PREP TIME: 10 TO 15 MINUTES

COOK TIME: 4 TO 5 HOURS (LOW) ■ 2 TO 2½ HOURS (HIGH)

- 1   stick unsalted butter, at room temperature
- 3   to 4 cloves garlic, minced
- 2   tablespoons finely minced fresh parsley
- 4   to 5 ears of corn, husked
      Salt and freshly ground black pepper to taste

1. Thoroughly mix together butter, garlic and parsley in small bowl.

2. Place each ear of corn on a piece of aluminum foil and generously spread butter on each ear. Season corn with salt and pepper and tightly seal foil. Place corn in the **CROCK-POT®** Slow Cooker; add enough water to come ¼ of the way up each ear. It is okay to overlap ears.

3. Cover; cook on LOW for 4 to 5 hours or on HIGH for 2 to 2½ hours or until done.

RED CABBAGE AND APPLES

Spiced Apple & Cranberry Compote

MAKES 6 SERVINGS

PREP TIME: 5 MINUTES

COOK TIME: 4 TO 5 HOURS (LOW)

2½ cups cranberry juice cocktail
1 package (6 ounces) dried apples
½ cup (2 ounces) dried cranberries
½ cup Rhine wine or apple juice
½ cup honey
2 cinnamon sticks, broken into halves
Frozen yogurt or ice cream (optional)
Additional cinnamon sticks (optional)

Mix juice, apples, cranberries, wine, honey and cinnamon stick halves in **CROCK-POT**® Slow Cooker. Cover and cook on LOW for 4 to 5 hours or until liquid is absorbed and fruit is tender. Remove and discard cinnamon stick halves. Ladle compote into bowls. Serve warm, at room temperature, or chilled with scoop of frozen yogurt or ice cream, and garnish with additional cinnamon sticks, if desired.

Pesto Rice and Beans

MAKES 8 SERVINGS

PREP TIME: 5 MINUTES

COOK TIME: 3 HOURS (LOW)

1 can (15 ounces) great Northern beans, rinsed and drained
1 can (14 ounces) chicken broth
¾ cup uncooked long-grain white rice
1½ cups frozen cut green beans, thawed and drained
½ cup prepared pesto
Grated Parmesan cheese (optional)

1. Combine beans, broth and rice in the **CROCK-POT**® Slow Cooker. Cover; cook on LOW for 2 hours.

2. Stir in green beans; cover and cook 1 hour or until rice and beans are tender. Turn off slow cooker and remove stoneware to heatproof surface. Stir in pesto and Parmesan cheese, if desired. Let stand, covered, 5 minutes or until cheese is melted. Serve immediately.

Wild Rice with Fruit & Nuts

MAKES 6 TO 8 SERVINGS

PREP TIME: 10 MINUTES

COOK TIME: 7 HOURS (LOW) ■ 2½ TO 3 HOURS (HIGH)

2	cups wild rice (or wild rice blend), rinsed*
½	cup dried cranberries
½	cup chopped raisins
½	cup chopped dried apricots
½	cup almond slivers, toasted
5	to 6 cups chicken broth
1	cup orange juice
2	tablespoons butter, melted
1	teaspoon ground cumin
2	green onions, thinly sliced
2	to 3 tablespoons chopped fresh parsley
	Salt and pepper to taste

*Do not use parboiled rice or a blend containing parboiled rice.

1. Combine wild rice, cranberries, raisins, apricots and almonds in the **CROCK-POT**® Slow Cooker.

2. Combine broth, orange juice, butter and cumin in medium bowl. Pour mixture over rice and stir to mix.

3. Cover; cook on LOW for 7 hours or on HIGH for 2½ to 3 hours. Stir once, adding more hot broth if necessary.

4. When rice is soft to the bite, add green onions and parsley. Adjust seasonings. Cook for 10 additional minutes and serve.

Fiesta Rice and Sausage

MAKES 10 TO 12 SERVINGS

PREP TIME: 10 MINUTES

COOK TIME: 4 TO 6 HOURS (LOW) ■ 2 TO 3 HOURS (HIGH)

2   pounds spicy Italian sausage, casings removed
2   cloves garlic, minced
2   teaspoons ground cumin
4   onions, chopped
4   green bell peppers, chopped
3   jalapeño peppers,* seeded and minced
4   cups beef broth
2   packages (6¼ ounces each) long grain and wild rice mix

*Jalapeño peppers can sting and irritate the skin; wear rubber gloves when handling peppers and do not touch eyes. Wash hands after handling.

1. Brown sausage on large nonstick skillet over medium-high heat, stirring to break up meat. Add garlic and cumin; cook and stir 30 seconds. Add onions, bell peppers and jalapeño peppers. Cook and stir 5 minutes until onions are tender. Place mixture into the **CROCK-POT**® Slow Cooker.

2. Stir in beef broth and rice.

3. Cover; cook on LOW for 4 to 6 hours or on HIGH for 2 to 3 hours.

Winter Squash and Apples

MAKES 4 TO 6 SERVINGS

PREP TIME: 15 MINUTES

COOK TIME: 6 TO 7 HOURS (LOW)

1   teaspoon salt
½   teaspoon pepper
1   butternut squash (about 2 pounds), peeled and seeded
2   apples, cored and cut into slices
1   medium onion, quartered and sliced
1½   tablespoons butter

1. Combine salt and pepper in small bowl; set aside.

2. Cut squash into 2-inch pieces; place in the **CROCK-POT**® Slow Cooker. Add apples and onion. Sprinkle with salt mixture; stir well. Cover; cook on LOW for 6 to 7 hours or until done.

3. Just before serving, stir in butter and season with additional salt and pepper.

Variation: Add ¼ to ½ cup brown sugar and ½ teaspoon cinnamon along with butter; mix well.

Donna's Potato Casserole

MAKES 8 TO SERVINGS

PREP TIME: 10 MINUTES

COOK TIME: 8 TO 10 HOURS (LOW) ■ 5 TO 6 HOURS (HIGH)

1	can (10¾ ounces) condensed cream of chicken soup, undiluted
1	cup (8 ounces) sour cream
¼	cup chopped onion
¼	cup plus 3 tablespoons butter, melted, divided
1	teaspoon salt
2	pounds potatoes, peeled and chopped
2	cups (8 ounces) shredded Cheddar cheese
1½	to 2 cups stuffing mix

1. Combine soup, sour cream, onion, ¼ cup butter and salt in small bowl.

2. Combine potatoes and cheese in the **CROCK-POT**® Slow Cooker. Pour soup mixture over potato mixture; mix well. Sprinkle stuffing mix over potato mixture; drizzle with remaining 3 tablespoons butter.

3. Cover; cook on LOW for 8 to 10 hours or on HIGH for 5 to 6 hours or until potatoes are tender.

Tip: Store raw potatoes in a cool, dark, dry, well-ventilated place. Do not refrigerate.

Sweet Endings

FRESH, TASTY DESSERTS FOR THE PERFECT FINISH

Cherry Flan

MAKES 6 SERVINGS

PREP TIME: 10 MINUTES

COOK TIME: 3½ TO 4 HOURS (LOW)

 5 eggs
 ½ cup sugar
 ½ teaspoon salt
 ¾ cup flour
 1 can (12 ounces) evaporated milk
 1 teaspoon vanilla
 1 bag (16 ounces) frozen pitted, dark sweet cherries, thawed
 Sweetened whipped cream or cherry vanilla ice cream

1. Grease the inside of the **CROCK-POT**® Slow Cooker stoneware with butter or nonstick cooking spray.

2. Beat eggs, sugar and salt in large bowl of electric mixer at high speed until thick. Add flour; beat until smooth. Beat in evaporated milk and vanilla.

3. Pour batter into prepared stoneware. Place cherries evenly over batter. Cover; cook on LOW for 3½ to 4 hours or until flan is set. Serve warm with whipped cream or ice cream.

Decadent Chocolate Delight

MAKES 12 SERVINGS

PREP TIME: 5 TO 10 MINUTES

COOK TIME: 6 TO 8 HOURS (LOW) ■ 3 TO 4 HOURS (HIGH)

1	package (about 18 ounces) chocolate cake mix
1	cup (8 ounces) sour cream
1	cup chocolate chips
1	cup water
4	eggs
¾	cup vegetable oil
1	package (4-serving size) instant chocolate pudding mix

1. Grease the inside of the **CROCK-POT**® Slow Cooker stoneware with butter or nonstick cooking spray.

2. Combine cake mix, sour cream, chocolate chips, water, eggs, oil and pudding mix in prepared stoneware; mix well.

3. Cover; cook on LOW for 6 to 8 hours or on HIGH for 3 to 4 hours. Serve hot or warm with ice cream.

HELPFUL HINTS

Keep these general guidelines in mind when making delicious desserts and baked goods in your **CROCK-POT**® Slow Cooker:

● Do not over-beat the batters of cakes and breads. Follow all recommended mixing times.

● Do not add water to the **CROCK-POT**® Slow Cooker unless instructed to do so in the recipe.

● After cakes and breads have finished cooking, allow them to cool in the stoneware for 5 minutes before removing.

Strawberry Rhubarb Crisp

MAKES 8 SERVINGS

PREP TIME: 20 MINUTES

COOK TIME: 1½ HOURS (HIGH) PLUS 15 TO 20 MINUTES (375°F OVEN)

FRUIT FILLING

4	cups hulled, sliced strawberries
4	cups diced rhubarb (about 5 stalks), ½-inch dice
1½	cups granulated sugar
2	tablespoons lemon juice
1½	tablespoons cornstarch, plus water (optional)

TOPPING

1	cup flour
1	cup oats (not instant)
½	cup granulated sugar
½	cup brown sugar
½	teaspoon ground ginger
½	teaspoon ground nutmeg
½	cup (1 stick) butter, cut into small pieces
½	cup sliced almonds, toasted*

***To toast almonds, spread in single layer on baking sheet. Bake in preheated 350°F oven for 8 to 10 minutes or until golden brown, stirring frequently.**

1. To make fruit filling: Grease the inside of the **CROCK-POT**® Slow Cooker stoneware with butter or nonstick cooking spray. Combine strawberries, rhubarb, sugar and lemon juice in a large bowl. Transfer mixture to prepared stoneware. Cover; cook on HIGH for 1½ hours or until fruit is tender.

2. If fruit is dry, add a little water. If fruit has too much liquid, mix cornstarch with a small amount of water and stir into the fruit. Cook for 15 additional minutes on HIGH. Preheat oven to 375°F.

3. To make topping: Combine flour, oats, sugars, ginger and nutmeg in a medium bowl. With fingertips, pinch the butter into the mixture to a pea-like consistency. Stir in almonds.

4. Remove lid; gently pour topping on fruit. Transfer stoneware to oven. Bake for 15 to 20 minutes or until topping begins to brown.

Fruit & Nut Baked Apples

MAKES 4 SERVINGS

PREP TIME: 10 MINUTES

COOK TIME: 3 TO 4 HOURS (LOW)

4	large baking apples, such as Rome Beauty or Jonathan
1	tablespoon lemon juice
⅓	cup chopped dried apricots
⅓	cup chopped walnuts or pecans
3	tablespoons packed light brown sugar
½	teaspoon ground cinnamon
2	tablespoons melted butter or margarine
	Caramel ice cream topping (optional)

1. Scoop out center of each apple, leaving 1½-inch-wide cavity about ½ inch from bottom. Peel top of apple down about 1 inch. Brush peeled edges evenly with lemon juice. Mix apricots, walnuts, brown sugar and cinnamon in small bowl. Add butter; mix well. Spoon mixture evenly into apple cavities.

2. Pour ½ cup water in bottom of **CROCK-POT**® Slow Cooker. Place 2 apples in bottom of cooker. Arrange remaining 2 apples above but not directly on top of bottom apples.

3. Cover; cook on LOW for 3 to 4 hours or until apples are tender. Serve warm or at room temperature with caramel ice cream topping, if desired.

Cook's Nook: Ever wonder why you need to brush lemon juice around the top of an apple? Citrus fruits contain an acid that keeps apples, potatoes and other white vegetables from discoloring once they are cut or peeled.

Apple-Date Crisp

MAKES 6 SERVINGS

PREP TIME: 20 TO 30 MINUTES

COOK TIME: 4 HOURS (LOW) ■ 2 HOURS (HIGH)

- 6 cups thinly sliced peeled apples (about 6 medium apples, preferably Golden Delicious)
- 2 teaspoons lemon juice
- ⅓ cup chopped dates
- 1⅓ cups uncooked quick oats
- ½ cup all-purpose flour
- ½ cup packed light brown sugar
- ½ teaspoon cinnamon
- ¼ teaspoon ground ginger
- ¼ teaspoon salt
  Dash ground nutmeg
- ¼ cup (½ stick) cold butter, cut into small pieces

1. Grease the inside of the **CROCK-POT**® Slow Cooker stoneware with butter or nonstick cooking spray. Place apples in medium bowl. Sprinkle with lemon juice; toss to coat. Add dates and mix well. Transfer apple mixture to prepared stoneware.

2. Combine oats, flour, brown sugar, cinnamon, ginger, salt and nutmeg in medium bowl. Cut in butter with pastry blender or two knives until mixture resembles coarse crumbs.

3. Sprinkle oats mixture over apples; smooth top. Cover; cook on LOW for 4 hours or on HIGH for 2 hours or until apples are tender.

"Peachy Keen" Dessert Treat

MAKES 8 TO 12 SERVINGS

PREP TIME: 10 TO 15 MINUTES

COOK TIME: 4 TO 6 HOURS (LOW)

- 1⅓ cups uncooked old-fashioned oats
- 1 cup granulated sugar
- 1 cup packed light brown sugar
- ⅔ cup buttermilk baking mix
- 2 teaspoons cinnamon
- ½ teaspoon ground nutmeg
- 2 pounds fresh peaches (about 8 medium), sliced

Grease the inside of the **CROCK-POT**® Slow Cooker stoneware with nonstick cooking spray. Combine oats, sugars, baking mix, cinnamon and nutmeg in large bowl. Stir in peaches until well blended; pour into prepared stoneware. Cover; cook on LOW for 4 to 6 hours or until done.

Streusel Pound Cake

MAKES 6 TO 8 SERVINGS

PREP TIME: 10 TO 15 MINUTES

COOK TIME: 3 TO 4 HOURS (HIGH)

- 1 package (16 ounces) pound cake mix, plus ingredients to prepare mix
- ¼ cup brown sugar
- 1 tablespoon flour
- ¼ cup nuts, chopped
- 1 teaspoon cinnamon

Grease the inside of the **CROCK-POT**® Slow Cooker stoneware with nonstick cooking spray. Prepare cake mix according to package directions; stir in brown sugar, flour, nuts and cinnamon. Pour batter into prepared stoneware. Cover; cook on HIGH for 3 to 4 hours or until done.

"PEACHY KEEN" DESSERT TREAT

Coconut Rice Pudding

MAKES 6 (¾-CUP) SERVINGS

PREP TIME: 30 TO 35 MINUTES

COOK TIME: 4 HOURS (LOW) ■ 2 HOURS (HIGH)

2	cups water
1	cup uncooked long-grain rice
1	tablespoon unsalted butter
	Pinch salt
18	ounces evaporated milk
1	can (14 ounces) cream of coconut
½	cup golden raisins
3	egg yolks, beaten
	Grated peel of 2 limes
1	teaspoon vanilla
	Toasted shredded coconut (optional)

1. Place water, rice, butter and salt in medium saucepan. Bring to rolling boil over high heat, stirring frequently. Reduce heat to low. Cover; cook for 10 to 12 minutes. Remove from heat; let stand, covered, for 5 minutes.

2. Grease the inside of the **CROCK-POT**® Slow Cooker stoneware with nonstick cooking spray. Add evaporated milk, cream of coconut, raisins, egg yolks, lime peel and vanilla to prepared stoneware; mix well. Add rice; stir to combine.

3. Cover; cook on LOW for 4 hours or on HIGH for 2 hours. Stir every 30 minutes, if possible. Pudding will thicken as it cools. Top with toasted coconut, if desired.

Pecan-Cinnamon Pudding Cake

MAKES 8 SERVINGS

PREP TIME: 20 MINUTES

COOK TIME: 2 TO 2½ HOURS (HIGH)

- ⅓ cup all-purpose flour
- ½ cup granulated sugar
- 1½ teaspoons baking powder
- 1½ teaspoons cinnamon
- ⅔ cup milk
- 5 tablespoons melted butter or margarine, divided
- 1 cup chopped pecans
- 1½ cups water
- ¾ cup packed brown sugar
- Whipped cream (optional)

1. Grease the inside of the **CROCK-POT**® Slow Cooker stoneware with butter or nonstick cooking spray. Stir together flour, granulated sugar, baking powder and cinnamon in medium bowl. Stir in milk and 3 tablespoons butter; mix just until blended. Stir in pecans. Spread on bottom of prepared stoneware.

2. Combine water, brown sugar, and remaining 2 tablespoons butter in small saucepan; bring to a boil. Pour over batter in slow cooker.

3. Cover; cook on HIGH for 2 to 2½ hours or until toothpick inserted into center of cake comes out clean. Let stand, uncovered, for 30 minutes. Serve warm with whipped cream, if desired.

Red Hot Applesauce

MAKES 6 SERVINGS

PREP TIME: 10 TO 15 MINUTES

COOK TIME: 7 TO 8 HOURS (LOW) ■ 4 HOURS (HIGH)

10 to 12 apples, peeled, cored and chopped
¾ cup hot cinnamon candies
½ cup apple juice or water

Combine apples, candies and apple juice in the **CROCK-POT**® Slow Cooker. Cover; cook on LOW for 7 to 8 hours or on HIGH for 4 hours or until desired consistency. Serve warm or chilled.

Bananas Foster

MAKES 12 SERVINGS

PREP TIME: 5 TO 10 MINUTES

COOK TIME: 1 TO 2 HOURS (LOW)

12 bananas, cut into quarters
1 cup flaked coconut
1 teaspoon cinnamon
½ teaspoon salt
1 cup dark corn syrup
⅔ cup butter, melted
2 teaspoons grated lemon peel
¼ cup lemon juice
2 teaspoons rum
12 slices pound cake
1 quart vanilla ice cream

Combine bananas and coconut in the **CROCK-POT**® Slow Cooker. In medium bowl, stir together cinnamon, salt, corn syrup, butter, lemon peel, lemon juice and rum; pour over bananas. Cover; cook on LOW for 1 to 2 hours. Pour warm sauce over pound cake slices topped with ice cream.

RED HOT APPLESAUCE

Peach-Pecan Upside-Down Cake

MAKES 10 SERVINGS

PREP TIME: 10 MINUTES

COOK TIME: 3 HOURS (HIGH)

- 1 can (8½ ounces) peach slices
- ⅓ cup packed brown sugar
- 2 tablespoons butter or margarine, melted
- ¼ cup chopped pecans
- 1 package (16 ounces) pound cake mix, plus ingredients to prepare mix
- ½ teaspoon almond extract
  Whipped cream (optional)

1. Generously grease 7½-inch cake pan or baking dish that will fit inside the **CROCK-POT**® Slow Cooker stoneware using butter or nonstick cooking spray; set aside.

2. Drain peach slices, reserving 1 tablespoon juice. Combine reserved peach juice, brown sugar and butter in prepared pan. Arrange peach slices on top of brown sugar mixture. Sprinkle with pecans.

3. Prepare cake mix according to package directions; stir in almond extract. Spread over peach mixture. Cover pan with lid or aluminum foil. Make foil handles (see below). Use foil handles to place pan into slow cooker. Cover; cook on HIGH for 3 hours.

4. Remove pan from slow cooker using foil handles. Cool pan, uncovered, on wire rack for 10 minutes. Run narrow spatula around sides of pan; invert onto serving plate. Serve warm with whipped cream, if desired.

Foil handles: Tear off three 18×2-inch strips of heavy foil or use regular foil folded to double thickness. Crisscross foil strips in spoke design and place pan on center of strips. Pull strips up and over pan.

Baked Ginger Apples

MAKES 4 SERVINGS

PREP TIME: 10 TO 15 MINUTES

COOK TIME: 4½ HOURS (LOW) ■ 2½ HOURS (HIGH)

4	large Red Delicious apples
½	cup (1 stick) unsalted butter, melted
⅓	cup chopped macadamia nuts
¼	cup chopped dried apricots
2	tablespoons finely chopped crystallized ginger
1	tablespoon dark brown sugar
¾	cup brandy
½	cup vanilla pudding mix
2	cups heavy cream

1. Slice tops off apples; remove cores. Combine butter, nuts, apricots, ginger and brown sugar in medium bowl. Fill apples with nut mixture. Place apples in the **CROCK-POT**® Slow Cooker. Pour brandy into slow cooker. Cover; cook on LOW for 4 hours or on HIGH for 2 hours.

2. Gently remove apples from slow cooker; keep warm. Combine pudding mix and cream in small bowl. Add to slow cooker; stir to combine with brandy. Turn slow cooker to HIGH, if needed. Cover; cook on HIGH 30 minutes. Stir until smooth. Return apples to slow cooker; keep warm. Serve apples with cream mixture.

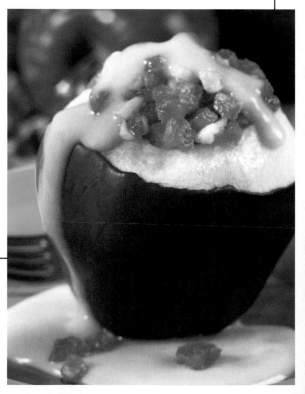

Gingerbread

MAKES 6 TO 8 SERVINGS

PREP TIME: 10 TO 15 MINUTES

COOK TIME: 3 TO 4 HOURS (HIGH)

½ cup butter, softened
½ cup sugar
1 egg, lightly beaten
1 cup light molasses
2½ cups all-purpose flour
1½ teaspoons baking soda
1 teaspoon cinnamon
2 teaspoons ground ginger
½ teaspoon ground cloves
½ teaspoon salt
1 cup hot water
   Whipped cream (optional)

1. Beat together butter and sugar in large bowl. Add egg, molasses, flour, baking soda, cinnamon, ginger, cloves and salt. Stir in hot water and mix well.

2. Grease the inside of the **CROCK-POT**® Slow Cooker stoneware with butter or nonstick cooking spray. Pour batter into prepared stoneware. Cover; cook on HIGH for 3 to 4 hours. Serve warm topped with whipped cream, if desired.

Steamed Pumpkin Cake

MAKES 12 SERVINGS

PREP TIME: 15 MINUTES

COOK TIME: 3 TO 3½ HOURS (HIGH)

1½	cups all-purpose flour
1½	teaspoons baking powder
1½	teaspoons baking soda
1	teaspoon ground cinnamon
½	teaspoon salt
¼	teaspoon ground cloves
½	cup unsalted butter, melted
2	cups packed light brown sugar
3	eggs, beaten
1	can (15 ounces) solid-pack pumpkin
	Sweetened whipped cream (optional)

1. Grease 2½-quart soufflé dish or baking pan that fits into slow cooker with butter or nonstick cooking spray.

2. Combine flour, baking powder, baking soda, cinnamon, salt and cloves in medium bowl; set aside.

3. Beat butter, brown sugar and eggs in large bowl with electric mixer at medium speed until creamy. Beat in pumpkin. Stir in flour mixture. Spoon batter into prepared soufflé dish.

4. Fill **CROCK-POT**® Slow Cooker with 1-inch hot water. Make foil handles, using technique described below, to allow for easy removal of soufflé dish. Place soufflé dish into slow cooker. Cover; cook on HIGH for 3 to 3½ hours or until wooden toothpick inserted into center comes out clean.

5. Use foil handles to lift dish from slow cooker. Cool on wire rack 15 minutes. Invert cake onto serving platter. Cut into wedges and serve with dollop of whipped cream, if desired.

Foil handles: Tear off three 18×2-inch strips of heavy foil or use regular foil folded to double thickness. Crisscross foil strips in spoke design and place soufflé dish on center of strips. Pull foil strips up and over dish.

Serving Suggestion: Enhance this old-fashioned dense cake with a topping of sautéed apples or pear slices, or a scoop of pumpkin ice cream.

Homestyle Apple Brown Betty

MAKES 8 SERVINGS

PREP TIME: 15 MINUTES

COOK TIME: 3 TO 4 HOURS (LOW) ■ 2 HOURS (HIGH)

6 cups cooking apples, peeled, cored and cut into eighths
1 cup bread crumbs
1 teaspoon ground cinnamon
1 teaspoon ground nutmeg
⅛ teaspoon salt
¾ cup packed brown sugar
½ cup butter or margarine, melted
¼ cup finely chopped walnuts

1. Lightly grease the **CROCK-POT**® Slow Cooker stoneware with butter or nonstick cooking spray. Place the apples on the bottom of the stoneware.

2. Combine the bread crumbs, cinnamon, nutmeg, salt, brown sugar, butter and walnuts. Spread over the apples in the stoneware.

3. Cover; cook on LOW for 3 to 4 hours or on HIGH for 2 hours.

Note: This recipe conjures up an amazing dessert out of simple ingredients.

Tip: For a 5-, 6- or 7-quart **CROCK-POT**® Slow Cooker, double all ingredients.

Brownie Bottoms

MAKES 6 SERVINGS

PREP TIME: 12 MINUTES

COOK TIME: 1½ HOURS (HIGH)

- ½ cup brown sugar
- ¾ cup water
- 2 tablespoons unsweetened cocoa powder
- 2½ cups packaged brownie mix
- 1 package (2¾ ounces) instant chocolate pudding mix
- ½ cup milk chocolate chips
- 2 eggs, beaten
- 3 tablespoons butter or margarine, melted

1. Lightly grease the inside of the **CROCK-POT**® Slow Cooker stoneware with butter or nonstick cooking spray. In a small saucepan, combine brown sugar, water and cocoa powder; bring to a boil.

2. Combine brownie mix, pudding mix, chocolate chips, eggs and butter in medium bowl; stir until well blended. Spread batter into prepared stoneware; pour boiling sugar mixture over batter. Cover; cook on HIGH for 1½ hours.

3. Turn off heat and let stand for 30 minutes. Serve warm.

Tip: For a 5-, 6- or 7-quart **CROCK-POT**® Slow Cooker, you may double all ingredients.

Serving suggestion: Serve this warm chocolate dessert with whipped cream or ice cream.

Chocolate Croissant Pudding

MAKES 6 SERVINGS

PREP TIME: 10 TO 15 MINUTES

COOK TIME: 3 TO 4 HOURS (LOW)

1½   **cups milk**
3   **eggs**
½   **cup sugar**
¼   **cup unsweetened cocoa powder**
½   **teaspoon vanilla**
¼   **teaspoon salt**
2   **plain croissants, cut into 1-inch pieces**
½   **cup chocolate chips**
   Whipped cream (optional)

1. Beat milk, eggs, sugar, cocoa powder, vanilla and salt in medium bowl.

2. Grease 1-quart casserole with butter or nonstick cooking spray. Layer half of croissants, chocolate chips and half of egg mixture in casserole. Repeat layers with remaining croissants and egg mixture.

3. Add rack to 5-quart **CROCK-POT**® Slow Cooker; pour in 1 cup water. Place casserole on rack (in place of rack, casserole may be propped up on a glass bowl or other dish). Cover; cook on LOW for 3 to 4 hours. Remove casserole from slow cooker. Serve with whipped cream, if desired.

Peach Cobbler

MAKES 4 TO 6 SERVINGS

PREP TIME: 10 MINUTES

COOK TIME: 2 HOURS (HIGH)

- **2** packages (16 ounces each) frozen peaches, thawed and drained
- **¾** cup plus 1 tablespoon sugar, divided
- **2** teaspoons cinnamon, divided
- **½** teaspoon ground nutmeg
- **¾** cup all-purpose flour
- **6** tablespoons butter, cut into small pieces
  Whipped cream (optional)

1. Combine peaches, ¾ cup sugar, 1½ teaspoons cinnamon and nutmeg in medium bowl. Place mixture in the **CROCK-POT**® Slow Cooker.

2. Combine flour, remaining sugar and remaining cinnamon in separate bowl. Cut in butter with pastry cutter or 2 knives until mixture resembles coarse crumbs. Sprinkle over peach mixture. Cover; cook on HIGH for 2 hours. Serve with whipped cream, if desired.

Family Fare

Simply put, slow cooking is the simplest way to cook. Add ingredients. Set the slow cooker. Walk away. Dinner is ready when you are'. It's this simplicity that makes your versatile **CROCK-POT**® Slow Cooker an ideal tool for involving kids in the cooking process:

- **Hands-on.** Young children can be your assistants and learn by doing.

- **Easy.** There are no complicated steps to follow, so kids don't lose interest.

- **Safe.** There are no open flames or hot burners to injure inexperienced cooks.

- **Satisfying.** Children can feel genuine pride in helping to nurture their family.

When kids help cook with a **CROCK-POT**® Slow Cooker, they get to experience first-hand the pleasure of preparing delicious foods. Plus, they are a lot more likely to eat—and enjoy—what's on the menu when they've had a hand in making it. That's a bonus for parents!

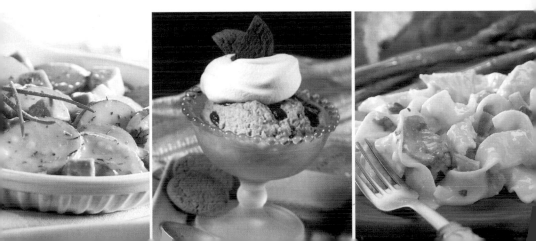

Everyday Favorites

FAST, FAMILY-PLEASING RECIPES FOR EVERY MEAL

Scalloped Potatoes & Ham

MAKES 5 TO 6 SERVINGS

PREP TIME: 5 TO 10 MINUTES

COOK TIME: 3½ HOURS (HIGH) PLUS 1 HOUR (LOW)

6   large russet potatoes, sliced into ¼-inch rounds
1   ham steak (about 1½ pounds), cut into cubes
1   can (10¾ ounces) condensed cream of mushroom soup
1   soup can water
4   ounces shredded Cheddar cheese
    Grill seasoning to taste

1. Grease the inside of the **CROCK-POT**® Slow Cooker stoneware with butter or nonstick cooking spray. Layer potatoes and ham in prepared stoneware.

2. In a large mixing bowl, combine soup, water, cheese and seasoning; pour over potatoes and ham.

3. Cover; cook on HIGH for about 3½ hours until potatoes are fork tender. ***Turn slow cooker to LOW*** and continue cooking for about 1 hour until done.

Mexican Cheese Soup

MAKES 6 TO 8 SERVINGS

PREP TIME: 20 TO 25 MINUTES

COOK TIME: 4 TO 5 HOURS (LOW) ■ 3 HOURS (HIGH)

- 1 pound processed cheese, cubed
- 1 pound ground beef, cooked and drained
- 1 can (8¾ ounces) whole kernel corn, undrained
- 1 can (15 ounces) kidney beans, undrained
- 1 jalapeño pepper, seeded and diced* (optional)
- 1 can (14½ ounces) diced tomatoes with green chilies, undrained
- 1 can (14½ ounces) stewed tomatoes, undrained
- 1 envelope taco seasoning
-    Corn chips (optional)

*Jalapeño peppers can sting and irritate the skin; wear rubber gloves when handling peppers and do not touch eyes. Wash hands after handling.

1. Grease the inside of the **CROCK-POT**® Slow Cooker stoneware with butter or nonstick cooking spray. Combine cheese, beef, corn, beans, jalapeño, if desired, tomatoes with chilies, stewed tomatoes and taco seasoning in prepared stoneware.

2. Cover; cook on LOW for 4 to 5 hours or on HIGH for 3 hours or until done. Serve with corn chips, if desired.

Chicken Tortilla Soup

MAKES 4 TO 6 SERVINGS

PREP TIME: 10 MINUTES

COOK TIME: 6 (LOW) ■ 3 HOURS (HIGH)

4	boneless, skinless chicken thighs
1	can (4 ounces) chopped mild green chilies, drained
2	cloves of garlic, minced
1	yellow onion, diced
2	cans (15 ounces each) diced tomatoes, undrained
½	to 1 cup chicken broth
1	teaspoon ground cumin
	Salt and black pepper to taste
2	tablespoons chopped fresh cilantro
4	corn tortillas, sliced into ¼-inch strips
½	cup shredded Monterey Jack cheese
1	avocado, peeled, diced and tossed with lime juice to prevent browning
	Juice of 1 lime

1. Place chicken in the **CROCK-POT**® Slow Cooker.

2. Combine chilies, garlic, onion, tomatoes, ½ cup broth and cumin in small bowl. Pour mixture over chicken.

3. Cover; cook on LOW for 6 hours or on HIGH for 3 hours until chicken is tender. Remove chicken; use 2 forks to shred the meat and return to slow cooker. Adjust seasonings, adding additional broth if necessary.

4. Just before serving, add cilantro and tortillas to slow cooker. Stir to blend.

5. Serve in soup bowls, topping each serving with cheese, avocado and a squeeze of lime juice.

Classic Spaghetti

MAKES 6 TO 8 SERVINGS

PREP TIME: 20 TO 30 MINUTES

COOK TIME: 6 TO 8 HOURS (LOW) ■ 3 TO 5 HOURS (HIGH)

- 2 tablespoons olive oil
- 2 onions, chopped
- 4 teaspoons minced garlic
- 2 green bell peppers, sliced
- 2 stalks celery, sliced
- 3 pounds ground beef
- 2 carrots, diced
- 1 cup mushrooms, sliced
- 1 can (28 ounces) tomato sauce
- 3 cups water
- 1 can (28 ounces) stewed tomatoes, undrained
- 1 tablespoon dried oregano
- 2 tablespoons minced parsley
- 2 teaspoons salt
- 2 teaspoons black pepper
- 1 tablespoon sugar
- 1 pound dry spaghetti

1. Heat oil in large skillet over medium-high heat. Add onion, garlic, green pepper and celery; sauté until tender. Place mixture in the **CROCK-POT**® Slow Cooker. In same skillet, brown ground beef. Drain and add to slow cooker.

2. Add carrots, mushrooms, tomato sauce, water, tomatoes with juice, oregano, parsley, salt, black pepper and sugar to slow cooker. Cover; cook on LOW for 6 to 8 hours or on HIGH for 3 to 5 hours or until done.

3. Cook spaghetti according to package directions; drain. Serve sauce over cooked spaghetti.

Honey Whole-Grain Bread

MAKES ABOUT 8 TO 10 SERVINGS

PREP TIME: 15 MINUTES

COOK TIME: 3 HOURS (HIGH)

- 3 cups whole wheat bread flour, divided
- 2 cups warm (not hot) whole milk
- ¾ to 1 cup all-purpose unbleached flour, divided
- ¼ cup honey
- 2 tablespoons vegetable oil
- 1 package active dry yeast
- ¾ teaspoon salt

1. Grease 1-quart high-sided baking pan that will fit in the **CROCK-POT**® Slow Cooker with butter or nonstick cooking spray. Set aside. Combine 1½ cups whole wheat flour, milk, ½ cup all-purpose flour, honey, oil, yeast and salt in large bowl. Beat with electric mixer at medium speed for 2 minutes.

2. Add remaining 1½ cups whole wheat flour and ¼ cup to ½ cup all-purpose flour until dough is no longer sticky. (If mixer has difficulty mixing dough, mix in remaining flours with wooden spoon.) Place in prepared pan.

3. Make foil handles (see page 138). Using foil handles, carefully place pan in slow cooker. Cover; cook on HIGH for 3 hours or until edges are browned.

4. Use foil handles to lift pan from slow cooker. Let stand 5 minutes. Remove bread from pan and place on wire rack to cool.

Barbecued Pulled Pork Sandwiches

MAKES ABOUT 8 SERVINGS

PREP TIME: 15 TO 20 MINUTES

COOK TIME: 12 TO 14 HOURS (LOW) ■ 6 TO 7 HOURS (HIGH)

- 1 pork shoulder roast (about 2½ pounds)
- 1 bottle (about 14 ounces) barbecue sauce
- 1 tablespoon fresh lemon juice
- 1 teaspoon brown sugar
- 1 medium onion, chopped
- 8 hamburger buns or hard rolls

1. Place pork roast in the **CROCK-POT**® Slow Cooker. Cover; cook on LOW for 10 to 12 hours or on HIGH for 5 to 6 hours.

2. Remove pork; shred meat with 2 forks. Discard any liquid in slow cooker. Return pork to slow cooker; add barbecue sauce, lemon juice, brown sugar and onion. Cover; cook on LOW for 2 hours or on HIGH for 1 hour longer.

3. Serve on hamburger buns or hard rolls.

Tip: For a 5-, 6- or 7-quart **CROCK-POT**® Slow Cooker, double all ingredients, except increase barbecue sauce to 21 ounces.

Serving suggestion: This kid-popular dish is sweet and savory and extremely easy to make. Serve with crunchy coleslaw on the side.

Banana Nut Bread

MAKES 6 SERVINGS

⅓ cup butter or margarine
⅔ cup sugar
2 eggs, well beaten
2 tablespoons dark corn syrup
3 ripe bananas, well mashed
1¾ cups all-purpose flour
2 teaspoons baking powder
½ teaspoon salt
¼ teaspoon baking soda
½ cup chopped walnuts

1. Grease and flour the inside of the **CROCK-POT**® Slow Cooker stoneware with butter or nonstick cooking spray. Cream butter in large bowl with electric mixer until fluffy. Slowly add sugar, eggs, corn syrup and mashed bananas. Beat until smooth.

2. Sift together flour, baking powder, salt and baking soda in small bowl. Slowly beat flour mixture into butter mixture. Add walnuts and mix thoroughly. Pour into prepared stoneware. Cover; cook on HIGH for 2 to 3 hours.

3. Let cool, then turn bread out onto serving platter.

Tip: For a 5-, 6- or 7-quart **CROCK-POT**® Slow Cooker, you may double all ingredients.

Variation: Add ½ cup chocolate chips for a delicious change of taste.

Note: Banana Nut Bread is a great way to use up overripe bananas. Not only is it delicious, but it also freezes well.

Three-Bean Turkey Chili

MAKES 6 TO 8 SERVINGS

PREP TIME: 10 TO 15 MINUTES

COOK TIME: 6 TO 8 HOURS (HIGH)

1   **pound ground turkey**
1   **small onion, chopped**
1   **can (28 ounces) diced tomatoes, undrained**
1   **can (15 ounces) garbanzo beans, rinsed and drained**
1   **can (15 ounces) kidney beans, rinsed and drained**
1   **can (15 ounces) black beans, rinsed and drained**
1   **can (8 ounces) tomato sauce**
1   **can (about 4 ounces) chopped mild green chilies**
1   **to 2 tablespoons chili powder**

1. Cook turkey and onion in medium skillet over medium-high heat, stirring to break up meat until turkey is no longer pink. Drain; place turkey mixture into the **CROCK-POT**® Slow Cooker.

2. Add tomatoes with juice, beans, tomato sauce, chilies and chili powder; mix well. Cover; cook on HIGH for 6 to 8 hours or until done.

Orange Date-Nut Bread

MAKES 8 TO 10 SERVINGS

PREP TIME: 10 TO 15 MINUTES

COOK TIME: 2½ HOURS (HIGH)

2	cups all-purpose unbleached flour
½	cup chopped pecans
1	teaspoon baking powder
½	teaspoon baking soda
¼	teaspoon salt
1	cup chopped dates
2	teaspoons dried orange peel
⅔	cup boiling water
¾	cup sugar
2	tablespoons shortening
1	egg, lightly beaten
1	teaspoon vanilla

1. Grease 1-quart high-sided baking pan that will fit in the **CROCK-POT®** Slow Cooker using butter or nonstick cooking spray; dust with flour. Set aside.

2. Combine flour, pecans, baking powder, baking soda and salt in medium bowl; set aside.

3. Combine dates and orange peel in separate medium bowl; pour boiling water over date mixture. Add sugar, shortening, egg and vanilla; stir just until blended.

4. Add flour mixture to date mixture; stir just until blended. Pour batter into prepared pan. Make foil handles (see page 138). Using foil handles, place pan in slow cooker. Cover; cook on HIGH for about 2½ hours until edges begin to brown.

5. Remove pan from slow cooker using foil handles. Cool on wire rack about 10 minutes; remove bread from pan and cool completely on rack.

Variation: Substitute 1 cup dried cranberries for dates.

Southwest Turkey Tenderloin Stew

MAKES 6 SERVINGS

PREP TIME: 5 MINUTES

COOK TIME: 5 TO 6 HOURS (LOW)

1½	pounds turkey tenderloins, cut into ¾-inch pieces
1	tablespoon chili powder
1	teaspoon ground cumin
¼	teaspoon salt
1	can (15 ounces) chili beans in spicy sauce, undrained
1	can (14½ ounces) chili-style stewed tomatoes, undrained
¾	cup prepared salsa or picante sauce
1	red bell pepper, cut into ¾-inch pieces
1	green bell pepper, cut into ¾-inch pieces
¾	cup chopped red or yellow onion
3	cloves garlic, minced
	Fresh cilantro (optional)

1. Place turkey in the **CROCK-POT**® Slow Cooker. Sprinkle with chili powder, cumin and salt; toss to coat.

2. Add beans, tomatoes with juice, salsa, bell peppers, onion and garlic; mix well. Cover; cook on LOW 5 to 6 hours.

3. Adjust seasonings, if desired. Ladle into bowls. Garnish with cilantro, if desired.

Hot & Juicy Reuben Sandwiches

MAKES 4 SERVINGS

PREP TIME: 25 MINUTES

COOK TIME: 7 TO 9 HOURS (LOW)

1	mild-cure corned beef (about 1½ pounds)
2	cups sauerkraut, drained
½	cup beef broth
1	small onion, sliced
1	clove garlic, minced
¼	teaspoon caraway seeds
4	to 6 peppercorns
8	slices pumpernickel or rye bread
4	slices Swiss cheese
	Mustard

1. Trim excess fat from corned beef. Place meat in the **CROCK-POT**® Slow Cooker. Add sauerkraut, broth, onion, garlic, caraway seeds and peppercorns.

2. Cover; cook on LOW for 7 to 9 hours.

3. Remove beef from slow cooker. Cut across the grain into 4 ½-inch-thick slices. Divide evenly among 4 slices bread. Top each slice with ½ cup drained sauerkraut mixture and one slice cheese. Spread mustard on remaining 4 bread slices. Close sandwich.

Note: This two-fisted stack of corned beef, sauerkraut and melted Swiss cheese makes a glorious sandwich you'll serve often.

Simple Turkey Soup

MAKES 8 SERVINGS

PREP TIME: 10 TO 15 MINUTES

COOK TIME: 3 TO 4 HOURS (HIGH)

2   pounds ground turkey, cooked and drained
1   can (28 ounces) whole tomatoes, undrained
2   cans (14 ounces each) beef broth
1   bag (16 ounces) frozen mixed soup vegetables
½   cup uncooked barley
1   teaspoon salt
1   teaspoon dried thyme
½   teaspoon ground coriander
    Dash black pepper

1. Combine turkey, tomatoes with juice, broth, vegetables, barley, salt, thyme, coriander and pepper in the **CROCK-POT**® Slow Cooker. Add water to cover.

2. Cover; cook on HIGH for 3 to 4 hours or until barley and vegetables are tender.

All-American Meatloaf

MAKES 6 TO 8 SERVINGS

PREP TIME: 10 TO 15 MINUTES

COOK TIME: 6 TO 8 HOURS (LOW) ■ 3 TO 4 HOURS (HIGH)

- 3 pounds ground beef
- 4 cups bread crumbs
- 2 cups ketchup
- 1 cup chopped onion
- 4 eggs, beaten
- 2 teaspoons salt
- 2 teaspoons black pepper
- 16 slices American cheese, cut into strips
- 1 can (6 ounces) tomato paste

1. In large mixing bowl, thoroughly combine beef, bread crumbs, ketchup, onion, eggs, salt and pepper. Shape ½ of mixture into loaf; top with cheese strips. Cover cheese with remaining meat, pressing edges together to seal.

2. Place meatloaf in the **CROCK-POT**® Slow Cooker; pour tomato paste over top. Cover; cook on LOW for 6 to 8 hours or on HIGH for 3 to 4 hours or until done.

Philly Cheese Steaks

MAKES 8 SERVINGS

PREP TIME: 10 TO 15 MINUTES

COOK TIME: 6 TO 8 HOURS (LOW)

2	pounds round steak, sliced
2	tablespoons butter or margarine, melted
4	onions, sliced
2	green bell peppers, sliced
1	tablespoon garlic-pepper seasoning blend
	Salt to taste
½	cup water
2	teaspoons beef bouillon granules
8	sandwich rolls
8	slices Cheddar cheese, cut in half

1. Combine steak, butter, onions, green pepper, garlic-pepper blend and salt in the **CROCK-POT**® Slow Cooker; stir to mix.

2. Whisk together water and bouillon in small bowl; pour into slow cooker. Cover; cook on LOW for 6 to 8 hours.

3. Remove meat, onions and green pepper from slow cooker and pile on sandwich rolls. Top with cheese and place under broiler until cheese is melted.

Oriental Chicken Wings

MAKES 32 SERVINGS

PREP TIME: 15 TO 20 MINUTES

COOK TIME: 5 TO 6 HOURS (LOW) ■ 2 TO 3 HOURS (HIGH)

16   chicken wings, split and tips removed
 1   cup chopped red onion
 1   cup soy sauce
 ¾   cup packed light brown sugar
 ¼   cup dry cooking sherry
 2   tablespoons chopped fresh ginger
 2   cloves garlic, minced
      Chopped fresh chives

1. Preheat broiler. Broil chicken wings for about 5 minutes per side. Transfer chicken to the **CROCK-POT**® Slow Cooker.

2. Combine onion, soy sauce, brown sugar, sherry, ginger and garlic in large bowl. Add to slow cooker; stir to blend well.

3. Cover and cook on LOW for 5 to 6 hours or on HIGH for 2 to 3 hours. Sprinkle with chives before serving.

Fiesta Black Bean Soup

MAKES 6 TO 8 SERVINGS

PREP TIME: 5 TO 10 MINUTES

COOK TIME: 8 TO 10 HOURS (LOW) ■ 4 TO 5 HOURS (HIGH)

6	cups chicken broth
12	ounces potatoes, peeled and diced
1	can (15 ounces) black beans, rinsed and drained
½	pound cooked ham, diced
½	onion, diced
1	can (4 ounces) chopped jalapeño peppers*
2	cloves garlic, minced
2	teaspoons dried oregano leaves
1½	teaspoons dried thyme leaves
1	teaspoon ground cumin
	Toppings: sour cream, chopped green bell pepper and chopped tomatoes

*Jalapeño peppers can sting and irritate the skin; wear rubber gloves when handling peppers and do not touch eyes. Wash hands after handling.

1. Combine broth, potatoes, beans, ham, onion, jalapeño peppers, garlic, oregano, thyme and cumin in the **CROCK-POT**® Slow Cooker; mix well.

2. Cover; cook on LOW 8 to 10 hours or on HIGH 4 to 5 hours.

3. Adjust seasonings. Serve with desired toppings.

Tarragon Turkey & Pasta

MAKES 4 SERVINGS

PREP TIME: 15 TO 20 MINUTES

COOK TIME: 6 TO 8 HOURS (LOW) ■ 3½ TO 4 HOURS (HIGH)

1½	to 2 pounds turkey tenderloins
½	cup thinly sliced celery
¼	cup thinly sliced green onions
4	tablespoons fresh tarragon, minced, divided
¼	cup dry white wine
1	teaspoon salt
1	teaspoon black pepper
½	cup plain yogurt
1	tablespoon fresh minced Italian parsley
1	tablespoon lemon juice
1½	tablespoons cornstarch
2	tablespoons water
4	cups pasta of your choice, cooked al denté

1. Combine the turkey, celery, green onions, 2 tablespoons fresh tarragon, wine, salt and pepper in the **CROCK-POT**® Slow Cooker. Mix thoroughly. Cover; cook on LOW for 6 to 8 hours or on HIGH for 3½ to 4 hours or until turkey is no longer pink.

2. Remove the turkey from the stoneware and cut it into ½-inch-thick medallions. Turn the **CROCK-POT**® Slow Cooker to HIGH. Add the yogurt, remaining 2 tablespoons fresh tarragon, parsley and lemon juice to the juices in the stoneware.

3. In a small bowl, combine the cornstarch and water. Add the mixture to the stoneware and cook until the juices thicken. Serve the turkey medallions over the pasta. Drizzle with the tarragon sauce.

Tip: For a 5-, 6- or 7-quart **CROCK-POT**® Slow Cooker, double all ingredients.

Parsnip and Carrot Soup

MAKES 4 SERVINGS

PREP TIME: 15 MINUTES

COOK TIME: 6 TO 9 HOURS (LOW) ■ 2 TO 4 HOURS (HIGH)

1	medium leek, thinly sliced
	Nonstick cooking spray
4	medium parsnips, peeled and diced
4	medium carrots, peeled and diced
4	cups fat-free chicken broth or stock
1	bay leaf
½	teaspoon salt
½	teaspoon black pepper
½	cup small pasta, cooked al denté and drained
1	tablespoon chopped Italian parsley
1	cup low-fat croutons

1. Cook the leek in a small nonstick skillet, sprayed with nonstick cooking spray, over medium heat until golden. Place in the **CROCK-POT**® Slow Cooker.

2. Add the parsnips, carrots, broth, bay leaf, salt and pepper. Cover; cook on LOW for 6 to 9 hours or on HIGH for 2 to 4 hours or until the vegetables are tender. Add the pasta during the last hour of cooking.

3. Remove bay leaf. Sprinkle each individual serving with parsley and croutons.

Note: This dish is a great year-round accompaniment to a main course of roasted meat. Or, the soup can stand alone as a quick, satisfying meal in its own right.

Tip: For a 5-, 6- or 7-quart **CROCK-POT**® Slow Cooker, double all ingredients.

Chicken and Sweet Potato Stew

MAKES 6 SERVINGS

PREP TIME: 15 MINUTES

COOK TIME: 6 TO 8 HOURS (LOW) ■ 3 TO 4 HOURS (HIGH)

4	boneless, skinless chicken breasts, cut into bite-size pieces
2	medium sweet potatoes, peeled and cubed
2	medium Yukon Gold potatoes, peeled and cubed
2	medium carrots, peeled and cut into ½-inch slices
1	can (28 ounces) whole stewed tomatoes
1	teaspoon salt
1	teaspoon paprika
1	teaspoon celery seeds
½	teaspoon black pepper
⅛	teaspoon ground cinnamon
⅛	teaspoon ground nutmeg
1	cup fat-free, low-sodium chicken broth
¼	cup fresh basil, chopped

1. Combine the chicken, potatoes, carrots, tomatoes, salt, paprika, celery seeds, pepper, cinnamon, nutmeg and broth in the **CROCK-POT**® Slow Cooker.

2. Cover; cook on LOW for 6 to 8 hours or on HIGH for 3 to 4 hours.

3. Sprinkle with basil just before serving.

Note: This light stew has an Indian influence and offers excellent flavor without the fat.

Tip: You may double all the ingredients when using a 5-, 6- or 7-quart **CROCK-POT**® Slow Cooker.

Bean and Corn Chili

MAKES 6 SERVINGS

PREP TIME: 15 TO 20 MINUTES

COOK TIME: 6 TO 8 HOURS (LOW) ■ 3 TO 4 HOURS (HIGH)

2	medium onions, finely chopped
5	cloves garlic, minced
½	teaspoon olive oil
2	tablespoons red wine
1	green bell pepper, seeded and finely chopped
1	red bell pepper, seeded and finely chopped
1	rib celery, finely sliced
6	Roma tomatoes, chopped
2	cans (15 ounces) kidney beans, rinsed and drained
1	can (6 ounces) tomato paste
1	cup frozen corn kernels
1	teaspoon salt
1	teaspoon chili powder
½	teaspoon black pepper
¼	teaspoon cumin
¼	teaspoon cayenne pepper
¼	teaspoon dried oregano
¼	teaspoon ground coriander
1½	cups fat-free chicken or vegetable broth

1. Cook the onions and garlic in the olive oil and red wine in a medium skillet until onions are tender. Add bell peppers, celery, tomatoes, beans, tomato paste, corn, salt, chili powder, black pepper, cumin, cayenne pepper, oregano, coriander and broth to the **CROCK-POT**® Slow Cooker. Mix thoroughly.

2. Cover; cook on LOW for 6 to 8 hours or on HIGH for 3 to 4 hours.

Note: Hearty yet low in fat, this chili will warm you on any winter evening.

Tip: For a 5-, 6- or 7-quart **CROCK-POT**® Slow Cooker, double all ingredients.

Classic Beef & Noodles

MAKES 8 SERVINGS

PREP TIME: 10 TO 15 MINUTES

COOK TIME: 8 TO 10 HOURS (LOW) ■ 4 TO 5 HOURS PLUS 30 MINUTES (HIGH)

1	tablespoon vegetable oil
2	pounds beef for stew, cut into 1-inch pieces
¼	pound mushrooms, sliced into halves
2	tablespoons chopped onion
2	cloves garlic, minced
1	teaspoon salt
1	teaspoon dried oregano leaves
½	teaspoon black pepper
¼	teaspoon dried marjoram leaves
1	bay leaf
1½	cups beef broth
⅓	cup dry sherry
1	cup (8 ounces) sour cream
½	cup all-purpose flour
¼	cup water
4	cups hot cooked noodles

1. Heat oil in large skillet. Brown beef on all sides. (Work in batches, if necessary.) Drain and discard fat.

2. Combine beef, mushrooms, onion, garlic, salt, oregano, pepper, marjoram and bay leaf in the **CROCK-POT**® Slow Cooker. Pour in beef broth and sherry. Cover; cook on LOW for 8 to 10 hours or on HIGH for 4 to 5 hours. Remove and discard bay leaf.

3. Combine sour cream, flour and water in small bowl. Stir about 1 cup liquid from slow cooker into sour cream mixture. Add mixture to slow cooker. Cook, uncovered, on HIGH 30 minutes or until thickened and bubbly. Serve over noodles.

Super Slow Sloppy Joes

MAKES 8 SERVINGS

PREP TIME: 15 TO 20 MINUTES

COOK TIME: 6 TO 8 HOURS (LOW)

3	pounds 90% lean ground beef
1	cup chopped onion
3	cloves garlic, minced
1¼	cups ketchup
1	cup chopped red bell pepper
5	tablespoons Worcestershire sauce
¼	cup brown sugar
3	tablespoons vinegar
3	tablespoons prepared mustard
2	teaspoons chili powder
	Hamburger buns

1. Brown ground beef, onion and garlic in large nonstick skillet over medium-high heat in two batches, stirring to separate meat. Drain and discard fat.

2. Combine ketchup, red pepper, Worcestershire sauce, brown sugar, vinegar, mustard and chili powder in the **CROCK-POT**® Slow Cooker. Stir in beef mixture.

3. Cover; cook on LOW for 6 to 8 hours or until done. Spoon onto hamburger buns.

Kids in the Kitchen

EASY, HANDS-ON RECIPES FOR ASPIRING YOUNG CHEFS

Mom's Tuna Casserole

MAKES 8 SERVINGS

PREP TIME: 10 MINUTES

COOK TIME: 5 TO 8 HOURS (LOW)

2 cans (12 ounces each) tuna, drained and flaked
3 cups diced celery
3 cups crushed potato chips, divided
6 hard-cooked eggs, chopped
1 can (10¾ ounces) condensed cream of mushroom soup
1 can (10¾ ounces) condensed cream of celery soup
1 cup mayonnaise
1 teaspoon dried tarragon
1 teaspoon black pepper

1. Combine tuna, celery, 2½ cups chips, eggs, soups, mayonnaise, tarragon and pepper in the **CROCK-POT**® Slow Cooker; stir well.

2. Cover; cook on LOW for 5 to 8 hours or until done.

3. Sprinkle with remaining ½ cup chips before serving.

Chicken Fiesta Soup

MAKES 8 SERVINGS

PREP TIME: 20 TO 30 MINUTES

COOK TIME: 8 HOURS (LOW)

4	boneless, skinless chicken breasts, cooked and shredded
1	can (14½ ounces) stewed tomatoes, drained
2	cans (4 ounces each) chopped green chilies
1	can (28 ounces) enchilada sauce
1	can (14½ ounces) chicken broth
1	cup finely chopped onions
2	cloves garlic, minced
1	teaspoon ground cumin
1	teaspoon chili powder
¾	teaspoon black pepper
1	teaspoon salt
¼	cup finely chopped fresh cilantro
1	cup frozen whole kernel corn
1	yellow squash, diced
1	zucchini, diced
8	tostada shells, crumbled
8	ounces shredded Cheddar cheese

1. Combine chicken, tomatoes, chilies, enchilada sauce, broth, onions, garlic, cumin, chili powder, pepper, salt, cilantro, corn, squash and zucchini in the **CROCK-POT**® Slow Cooker.

2. Cover; cook on LOW for 8 hours. To serve, fill individual bowls with soup. Garnish with crumbled tostada shells and cheese.

Easiest Chicken & Biscuits

MAKES 4 SERVINGS

PREP TIME: 10 MINUTES

COOK TIME: 4 TO 6 HOURS (LOW)

2 cups cooked chicken, cubed
1 can (10¾ ounces) condensed cream of mushroom soup
1 can (10¾ ounces) condensed cream of chicken soup
2 soup cans water
2 teaspoons chicken bouillon granules
½ teaspoon black pepper
1 can (8-pack) refrigerated buttermilk biscuits

Combine chicken cubes, soups, water, bouillon and pepper in the **CROCK-POT**® Slow Cooker. Cut biscuits into quarters; stir into mixture. Cover; cook on LOW for 4 to 6 hours, stirring occasionally, until done.

Macaroni and Cheese

MAKES 6 TO 8 SERVINGS

PREP TIME: 10 TO 15 MINUTES

COOK TIME: 2 TO 3 HOURS (HIGH)

6 cups cooked macaroni
2 tablespoons butter
4 cups evaporated milk
6 cups Cheddar cheese, shredded
2 teaspoons salt
½ teaspoon black pepper

In large mixing bowl, toss macaroni with butter. Stir in evaporated milk, cheese, salt and pepper; place in the **CROCK-POT**® Slow Cooker. Cover; cook on HIGH for 2 to 3 hours.

Variations: Make this mac 'n cheese recipe more fun. Add some tasty mix-ins: diced green or red bell pepper, peas, hot dog slices, chopped tomato, browned ground beef or chopped onion. Be creative!

EASIEST CHICKEN & BISCUITS

Slow Cooker Steak Fajitas

MAKES 4 SERVINGS

PREP TIME: 20 MINUTES

COOK TIME: 6 TO 7 HOURS (LOW)

1	beef flank steak (about 1 pound)
1	medium onion, cut into strips
½	cup medium salsa
2	tablespoons fresh lime juice
2	tablespoons chopped fresh cilantro
2	cloves garlic, minced
1	tablespoon chili powder
1	teaspoon ground cumin
½	teaspoon salt
1	small green bell pepper, cut into strips
1	small red bell pepper, cut into strips
	Flour tortillas, warmed
	Additional salsa

1. Cut flank steak lengthwise in half, then crosswise into thin strips. Combine onion, ½ cup salsa, lime juice, cilantro, garlic, chili powder, cumin and salt in the **CROCK-POT**® Slow Cooker.

2. Cover; cook on LOW for 5 to 6 hours. Add peppers. Cover; cook on LOW for 1 hour.

3. Serve with flour tortillas and additional salsa.

Sweet & Saucy Ribs

MAKES 4 SERVINGS

PREP TIME: 10 MINUTES

COOK TIME: 6 TO 8 HOURS (LOW)

2	pounds pork baby back ribs
1	teaspoon black pepper
2½	cups barbecue sauce (not mesquite flavored)
1	jar (8 ounces) cherry jam or preserves
1	tablespoon Dijon mustard
¼	teaspoon salt
	Additional salt and black pepper (optional)

1. Trim excess fat from ribs. Rub 1 teaspoon pepper over ribs. Cut ribs into 2-rib portions; place in the **CROCK-POT**® Slow Cooker.

2. Combine barbecue sauce, jam, mustard and ¼ teaspoon salt in small bowl; pour over ribs.

3. Cover; cook on LOW for 6 to 8 hours or until ribs are tender. Season with additional salt and pepper, if desired. Serve ribs with sauce.

Pumpkin-Cranberry Custard

MAKES 4 TO 6 SERVINGS

PREP TIME: 10 MINUTES

COOK TIME: 4 TO 4½ HOURS (HIGH)

1   can (30 ounces) pumpkin pie filling
1   can (12 ounces) evaporated milk
1   cup dried cranberries
4   eggs, beaten
1   cup crushed or whole ginger snap cookies (optional)
    Whipped cream (optional)

Combine pumpkin, evaporated milk, cranberries and eggs in the **CROCK·POT**® Slow Cooker; mix thoroughly. Cover; cook on HIGH for 4 to 4½ hours or until done. Serve with crushed or whole ginger snaps and whipped cream, if desired.

Pear Crunch

MAKES 4 SERVINGS

PREP TIME: 10 TO 15 MINUTES

COOK TIME: 3½ TO 4½ HOURS (LOW)

1   can (8 ounces) crushed pineapple in juice, undrained
¼   cup pineapple or apple juice
3   tablespoons dried cranberries
1½   teaspoons quick-cooking tapioca
¼   teaspoon vanilla extract
2   pears, cored and cut into halves
¼   cup granola with almonds

Combine undrained pineapple, juice, cranberries, tapioca and vanilla in the **CROCK·POT**® Slow Cooker; mix well. Place pears, cut side down, over pineapple mixture. Cover; cook on LOW for 3½ to 4½ hours. Arrange pear halves on serving plates. Spoon pineapple mixture over pear halves. Garnish with granola.

PUMPKIN-CRANBERRY CUSTARD

Chunky Sweet Spiced Apple Butter

MAKES 2 CUPS

PREP TIME: 15 MINUTES

COOK TIME: 8 HOURS (LOW)

4	cups peeled, chopped Granny Smith apples (about 1¼ pounds)
¾	cup packed dark brown sugar
2	tablespoons balsamic vinegar
4	tablespoons butter, divided
1	tablespoon cinnamon
½	teaspoon salt
¼	teaspoon ground cloves
1½	teaspoons vanilla extract

Combine apples, sugar, vinegar, 2 tablespoons butter, cinnamon, salt and cloves in the **CROCK-POT**® Slow Cooker. Cover; cook on LOW for 8 hours. Stir in remaining 2 tablespoons butter and vanilla. Cool completely.

"Wake Up to Health" Cereal

MAKES 6 SERVINGS

PREP TIME: 10 MINUTES

COOK TIME: 8 HOURS (LOW)

1½	cups uncooked steel-cut or old-fashioned oats
3	cups water
2	cups peeled, chopped apples
¼	cup sliced almonds
½	teaspoon cinnamon

Combine uncooked oats, water, apples, almonds and cinnamon in the **CROCK-POT**® Slow Cooker. Cover; cook on LOW for 8 hours.

CHUNKY SWEET SPICED APPLE BUTTER

The Best Beef Stew

MAKES 8 SERVINGS

PREP TIME: 20 MINUTES

COOK TIME: 8 TO 12 HOURS (LOW) ■ 4 TO 6 HOURS (HIGH)

½ cup plus 2 tablespoons all-purpose flour, divided
2 teaspoons salt
1 teaspoon black pepper
3 pounds beef for stew, cut into 1-inch pieces
1 can (16 ounces) diced tomatoes, undrained
3 potatoes, peeled and diced
½ pound smoked sausage, sliced
1 cup chopped leek
1 cup chopped onion
4 ribs celery, sliced
½ cup chicken broth
3 cloves garlic, minced
1 teaspoon dried thyme
3 tablespoons water

1. Combine ½ cup flour, salt and pepper in resealable plastic food storage bag. Add beef; shake bag to coat beef. Place beef in the **CROCK-POT**® Slow Cooker. Add tomatoes with juice, potatoes, sausage, leek, onion, celery, broth, garlic and thyme; stir well.

2. Cover; cook on LOW for 8 to 12 hours or on HIGH for 4 to 6 hours. *One hour before serving, turn slow cooker to HIGH.* Whisk together remaining 2 tablespoons flour and water in small bowl; stir into slow cooker. Cover; cook until thickened.

HELPFUL HINTS

You can cook frozen meats in the **CROCK-POT**® Slow Cooker if you follow these guidelines:

- Do not preheat slow cooker.

- Add at least 1 cup warm liquid to slow cooker before adding meat.

- Cook recipes an additional 4 to 6 hours on LOW or 2 hours on HIGH.

Triple Delicious Hot Chocolate

MAKES 6 SERVINGS

PREP TIME: 10 MINUTES

COOK TIME: 2¼ HOURS (LOW)

⅓ cup sugar

¼ cup unsweetened cocoa powder

¼ teaspoon salt

3 cups milk, divided

¾ teaspoon vanilla extract

1 cup heavy cream

1 square (1 ounce) bittersweet chocolate

1 square (1 ounce) white chocolate

¾ cup whipped cream

6 teaspoons mini chocolate chips or shaved bittersweet chocolate

1. Combine sugar, cocoa powder, salt and ½ cup milk in medium bowl. Beat until smooth. Pour into the **CROCK-POT**® Slow Cooker. Add remaining 2½ cups milk and vanilla. Cover; cook on LOW for 2 hours.

2. Add cream. Cover; cook on LOW for 10 to 15 minutes. Stir in bittersweet and white chocolates until melted.

3. Pour hot chocolate into 6 cups. Top each with 2 tablespoons whipped cream and 1 teaspoon chocolate chips.

One Big Cookie

MAKES 6 SERVINGS

PREP TIME: 15 TO 20 MINUTES

COOK TIME: 3 HOURS (LOW)

2	cups all-purpose flour
½	teaspoon salt
1	teaspoon baking powder
1	cup butter, at room temperature
1	cup packed brown sugar
¾	cup granulated sugar
2	eggs
1	teaspoon vanilla extract
1½	cups chocolate chips

1. Sift together flour, salt and baking powder; set aside.

2. Beat butter and sugars in large mixing bowl with electric mixer until creamy. Add eggs and vanilla; mix to incorporate. Slowly add flour mixture; mix until well incorporated. Stir in chocolate chips with spoon.

3. Grease the inside of the **CROCK-POT**® Slow Cooker stoneware with butter or nonstick cooking spray. Pour the batter into prepared stoneware.

4. Cover; cook on LOW for 3 hours or until clean knife inserted into center comes out clean.

Southwestern Stuffed Peppers

MAKES 4 SERVINGS

PREP TIME: 15 MINUTES

COOK TIME: 4 TO 6 HOURS (LOW)

- **4** green and/or red bell peppers
- **1** can (15 ounces) black beans, rinsed and drained
- **1** cup (4 ounces) shredded Pepper-Jack cheese
- **¾** cup medium salsa
- **½** cup frozen whole kernel corn
- **½** cup chopped green onions with tops
- **⅓** cup uncooked long grain converted rice
- **1** teaspoon chili powder
- **½** teaspoon ground cumin
  Sour cream (optional)

1. Cut thin slice off top of each pepper. Carefully remove seeds, leaving pepper whole.

2. Combine beans, cheese, salsa, corn, onions, rice, chili powder and cumin in medium bowl. Spoon filling evenly into each pepper. Place peppers in the **CROCK-POT**® Slow Cooker.

3. Cover; cook on LOW for 4 to 6 hours. Serve with sour cream, if desired.

Triple Chocolate Fantasy

MAKES 36 PIECES

PREP TIME: 10 MINUTES

COOK TIME: 1 HOUR (HIGH) PLUS 1 HOUR (LOW)

> 2 pounds white almond bark, broken into pieces
> 1 bar (4 ounces) German chocolate, broken into pieces
> 1 package (12 ounces) semi-sweet chocolate chips
> 3 cups lightly toasted, coarsely chopped pecans

1. Place chocolates in the **CROCK-POT**® Slow Cooker. Cover; cook on HIGH for 1 hour. Do not stir.

2. *Turn slow cooker to LOW.* Continue cooking for 1 hour, stirring every 15 minutes. Stir in nuts.

3. Drop mixture by tablespoonfuls onto baking sheet covered with waxed paper; let cool. Store in tightly covered container.

Variations: Here are a few ideas for other imaginative add-ins :

- raisins
- crushed peppermint candy
- candy-coated baking bits
- crushed toffee
- peanuts or pistachios

- chopped gum drops
- chopped dried fruit
- candied cherries
- chopped marshmallows
- sweetened coconut

Mulled Apple Cider

MAKES 10 SERVINGS

PREP TIME: 10 MINUTES

COOK TIME: 2½ TO 3 HOURS (HIGH)

- 2 quarts bottled apple cider or juice (not unfiltered)
- ¼ cup packed light brown sugar
- 1 square (8 inches) double-thickness cheesecloth
- 8 allspice berries
- 4 cinnamon sticks, broken into halves
- 12 whole cloves
- 1 large orange
  Additional cinnamon sticks (optional)

1. Combine apple cider and brown sugar in **CROCK-POT**® Slow Cooker. Rinse cheesecloth; squeeze out water. Wrap allspice berries and cinnamon stick halves in cheesecloth; tie securely with cotton string or strip of cheesecloth. Stick cloves randomly into orange; cut orange into quarters. Place spice bag and orange quarters in cider mixture.

2. Cover; cook on HIGH for 2½ to 3 hours.

3. Once cooked, cider may be turned to LOW and kept warm up to 3 additional hours. Remove and discard spice bag and orange before serving. Ladle cider into mugs. Garnish with additional cinnamon sticks, if desired.

Tip: To make inserting cloves into the orange a little easier, first pierce the orange skin with the point of wooden skewer. Remove the skewer and insert a clove.

Cashew Chicken

MAKES 6 SERVINGS

PREP TIME: 5 TO 10 MINUTES

COOK TIME: 6 TO 8 HOURS (LOW) ■ 4 TO 6 HOURS (HIGH)

6	chicken breasts
2	tablespoons butter
¼	cup chopped green onion
1	cup sliced mushrooms
1	can (10¾ ounces) condensed cream of mushroom soup
1	cup sliced celery
1½	tablespoons soy sauce
1½	cup cashews

Combine chicken, butter, green onion, mushrooms, soup, celery, soy sauce and cashews in the **CROCK-POT**® Slow Cooker. Cover; cook on LOW for 6 to 8 hours or on HIGH for 4 to 6 hours or until done.

HELPFUL HINTS

Time spent in the kitchen cooking with your kids is time well spent. You can share the value of preparing wholesome, comforting, nurturing foods while equipping them with the skills to create their own food traditions in the future. Even young children can participate in family meal preparation. Just remember these basics:

● Always make sure children are well-supervised in the kitchen.

● Only adults should use sharp utensils, plug in or turn on electric appliances or handle hot foods.

● Be sure to only assign tasks that the child can do and feel good about.

Mixed Berry Cobbler

MAKES 8 SERVINGS

PREP TIME: 10 MINUTES

COOK TIME: 4 HOURS (LOW)

1	package (16 ounces) frozen mixed berries
¾	cup granulated sugar
2	tablespoons quick-cooking tapioca
2	teaspoons grated lemon peel
1½	cups all-purpose flour
½	cup packed brown sugar
2¼	teaspoons baking powder
¼	teaspoon ground nutmeg
¾	cup milk
⅓	cup butter, melted
	Ice cream (optional)

1. Stir together berries, granulated sugar, tapioca and lemon peel in the **CROCK-POT**® Slow Cooker.

2. Combine flour, brown sugar, baking powder and nutmeg in medium bowl. Add milk and butter; stir just until blended. Drop spoonfuls on top of berry mixture.

3. Cover; cook on LOW for 4 hours. Uncover; let stand about 30 minutes. Serve with ice cream, if desired.

Turkey and Macaroni

MAKES 4 TO 6 SERVINGS

PREP TIME: 10 MINUTES

COOK TIME: 6 TO 8 HOURS (LOW) ■ 3 TO 4 HOURS (HIGH)

- 1 teaspoon vegetable oil
- 1½ pounds lean ground turkey
- 2 cans (10¾ ounces each) condensed tomato soup, undiluted
- 1 can (16 ounces) corn, drained
- ½ cup chopped onion
- 1 can (4 ounces) sliced mushrooms, drained
- 2 tablespoons ketchup
- 1 tablespoon mustard
- Salt and black pepper to taste
- 2 cups uncooked macaroni, cooked and drained

1. Heat oil in large nonstick skillet over medium-high heat; brown turkey, stirring to break up meat. Transfer turkey to **CROCK-POT**® Slow Cooker.

2. Add soup, corn, onion, mushrooms, ketchup, mustard, salt and pepper to slow cooker; mix well. Cover; cook on LOW for 6 to 8 hours or on HIGH for 3 to 4 hours.

3. Stir in macaroni. Cover; cook on LOW 30 minutes.

3-Cheese Chicken & Noodles

MAKES 6 SERVINGS

PREP TIME: 10 MINUTES

COOK TIME: 6 TO 10 HOURS (LOW) ■ 3 TO 4 HOURS (HI

3	cups chopped cooked chicken
1½	cups cottage cheese
1	can (10¾ ounces) condensed cream of chicken soup
1	package (8 ounces) wide egg noodles, cooked and drained
1	cup grated Monterey Jack cheese
½	cup diced celery
½	cup diced onion
1	cup diced green and/or red bell pepper
½	cup grated Parmesan cheese
½	cup chicken broth
1	can (4 ounces) sliced mushrooms, drained
2	tablespoons butter, melted
½	teaspoon dried thyme

Combine chicken, cottage cheese, soup, noodles, Monterey Jack cheese, celery, onion, peppers, Parmesan cheese, broth, mushroom butter and thyme in the **CROCK-POT**® Slow Cooker. Stir to coat ever Cover; cook on LOW for 6 to 10 hours or on HIGH for 3 to 4 hours.

Cheesy Pork and Potatoes

MAKES 6 SERVINGS

PREP TIME: 20 MINUTES

COOK TIME: 3 TO 5 HOURS (LOW)

½ pound ground pork, cooked and crumbled
½ cup finely crushed saltine crackers
⅓ cup barbecue sauce
1 egg
3 tablespoons butter or margarine
1 tablespoon vegetable oil
4 potatoes, peeled and thinly sliced
1 onion, thinly sliced
1 cup shredded mozzarella cheese
⅔ cup evaporated milk
1 teaspoon salt
¼ teaspoon paprika
⅛ teaspoon black pepper
Chopped fresh parsley

1. Combine pork, crackers, barbecue sauce and egg in large bowl; shape mixture into 6 patties. Set aside.

2. Heat margarine and oil in medium skillet. Cook and stir potatoes and onion until lightly browned. Drain. Place in **CROCK-POT**® Slow Cooker.

3. Combine cheese, milk, salt, paprika and pepper in small bowl. Pour into slow cooker. Layer pork patties on top. Cover; cook on LOW for 3 to 5 hours. Garnish with parsley.

Index

3-Cheese Chicken & Noodles ... 216

All-American Meatloaf 172
Apple-Date Crisp 131
Arroz con Queso 92
Asian-Spiced Chicken Wings 80
Asparagus and Cheese 94

Baked Ginger Apples 140
Banana Nut Bread 162
Bananas Foster 136
Barbecued Pulled Pork
    Sandwiches 160
Barley Beef Stroganoff 50
Bean and Corn Chili 184

BEEF
    All-American Meatloaf 172
    Barley Beef Stroganoff 50
    Beef Bourguignonne 88
    Carne Rellenos 58
    Classic Beef & Noodles 186
    Classic Spaghetti 158
    German-Style Bratwurst 56
    Hot & Juicy Reuben
        Sandwiches 168
    Korean BBQ Beef Short Ribs ... 74
    Maple-Glazed Meatballs 36
    Mexican Cheese Soup 154
    Philly Cheese Steaks 173
    Simple Coq au Vin 82
    Slow Cooker Steak Fajitas 196

Slow-Simmered Curried
    Chicken 90
Southwestern Stuffed
    Peppers 206
Spicy Sweet & Sour
    Mini-Franks 39
Super Slow Sloppy Joes 188
The Best Beef Stew 202
Wild Mushroom Beef Stew 40

Beef Bourguignonne 88
Best Asian-Style Ribs 56
Breakfast Bake 18
Breakfast Berry Bread Pudding ... 20
Brownie Bottoms 146

Cajun Chicken and Shrimp
    Creole 44
Caponata 102
Caribbean Sweet Potato & Bean
    Stew 66
Carne Rellenos 58
Cashew Chicken 211
Chai Tea 25
Cherry Flan 124
Cheesy Pork and Potatoes 218

CHICKEN
    3-Cheese Chicken &
        Noodles 216
    Cajun Chicken and Shrimp
        Creole 44
    Cashew Chicken 211

Chicken and Sweet Potato
Stew 182

Chicken Fiesta Soup 192

Chicken Provençal 78

Chicken Tortilla Soup 156

Easiest Chicken & Biscuits. . . . 194

Forty-Clove Chicken 86

Herbed Artichoke Chicken 52

Mediterranean Chicken 62

Moroccan Chicken Tagine 64

Oriental Chicken Wings. 174

Quatro Frijoles Con Pollo
Cantara 77

Stuffed Chicken Breasts 32

Thai Chicken 54

Chicken and Sweet Potato
Stew 182

Chicken Fiesta Soup 192

Chicken Provençal 78

Chicken Tortilla Soup 156

Chocolate Chip Lemon Loaf 22

Chocolate Croissant Pudding. . . . 148

Chunky Sweet Spiced Apple
Butter 200

Cioppino. 60

Classic Beef & Noodles 186

Classic Spaghetti 158

Coconut Rice Pudding. 134

Corn on the Cob with Garlic Herb
Butter 112

Country Sausage and Bean
Soup 48

Cran-Cherry Bread Pudding 28

Cran-Orange Acorn Squash 30

Creamy Curried Spinach 96

Decadent Chocolate Delight 126

Deluxe Potato Casserole 24

DESSERTS & BREADS

Apple-Date Crisp 131

Baked Ginger Apples. 140

Banana Nut Bread 162

Bananas Foster 136

Breakfast Berry Bread
Pudding. 20

Brownie Bottoms 146

Cherry Flan. 124

Chocolate Chip Lemon Loaf. . . . 22

Chocolate Croissant
Pudding. 148

Coconut Rice Pudding. 134

Cran-Cherry Bread Pudding . . . 28

Decadent Chocolate
Delight. 126

Fruit & Nut Baked Apples 130

Gingerbread. 141

Homestyle Apple Brown
Betty. 144

Honey Whole-Grain Bread 159

Mixed Berry Cobbler 212

One Big Cookie. 205

Orange Date-Nut Bread 166

Peach Cobbler 150

Peach-Pecan Upside-Down
Cake. 138

"Peachy Keen" Dessert
Treat 132

Pear Crunch. 198

Pecan-Cinnamon Pudding
Cake. 135

Poached Pears with Raspberry
Sauce. 35

Pumpkin-Cranberry
   Custard 198
Red Hot Applesauce 136
Spicy Fruit Dessert. 12
Steamed Pumpkin Cake 142
Strawberry Rhubarb Crisp 128
Streusel Pound Cake 132
Triple Chocolate Fantasy 208

Donna's Potato Casserole 122

Easiest Chicken & Biscuits. 194
Escalloped Corn 109

Fall-Apart Pork Roast 14
Fiesta Black Bean Soup 176
Fiesta Rice and Sausage 118
Forty-Clove Chicken 86
Fresh Herbed Turkey Breast 46
Fruit & Nut Baked Apples. 130

German-Style Bratwurst 56
Gingerbread. 141

Herbed Artichoke Chicken 52
Herbed Fall Vegetables 17
Homestyle Apple Brown
   Betty 144
Honey Whole-Grain Bread. 159
Hot & Juicy Reuben
   Sandwiches 168
Hot Broccoli Cheese Dip 39

Korean BBQ Beef Short Ribs 74

Macaroni and Cheese. 194

Maple-Glazed Meatballs 36
Mediterranean Chicken 62
Mediterranean Stew 84
Mexican Cheese Soup 154
Mixed Berry Cobbler 212
Mom's Tuna Casserole 190
Moroccan Chicken Tagine 64
Mulled Apple Cider. 210

One Big Cookie. 205
Orange Date-Nut Bread 166
Orange-Spiced Sweet
   Potatoes 106
Oriental Chicken Wings. 174

Parsnip and Carrot Soup. 180
Peach Cobbler 150
Peach-Pecan Upside-Down
   Cake 138
"Peachy Keen" Dessert Treat 132
Pear Crunch 198
Pecan-Cinnamon Pudding
   Cake 135
Pesto Rice and Beans. 115
Philly Cheese Steaks 173
Pizza Fondue 38
Poached Pears with Raspberry
   Sauce 35
Polenta-Style Corn Casserole. 71

PORK
Barbecued Pulled Pork
   Sandwiches. 160
Best Asian-Style Ribs 56
Cheesy Pork and Potatoes. . . . 218
Fall-Apart Pork Roast 14

Fiesta Rice and Sausage 118

Pizza Fondue. 38

Pork Loin with Sherry and
  Red Onions 42

Scalloped Potatoes & Ham . . . 152

Spicy Sweet & Sour
  Mini-Franks 39

Sweet & Saucy Ribs 197

Pork Loin with Sherry and Red
  Onions 42

Pumpkin-Cranberry Custard 198

Quatro Frijoles Con Pollo
  Cantara. 77

Ratatouille with Garbanzo
  Beans 72

Red Cabbage and Apples. 112

Red Hot Applesauce 136

Risi Bisi 76

Risotto-Style Peppered Rice 16

Roasted Tomato-Basil Soup 34

Scalloped Potatoes & Ham 152

Scalloped Potatoes and Parsnips. 110

Scalloped Tomatoes and Corn 31

SEAFOOD

Cajun Chicken and Shrimp
  Creole 44

Cioppino. 60

Mom's Tuna Casserole 190

Slow-Simmered Jambalaya. . . . 87

Simple Coq au Vin. 82

Simple Turkey Soup 170

Slow Cooker Steak Fajitas. 196

Slow-Simmered Curried Chicken . 90

Slow-Simmered Jambalaya 87

SOUPS & SIDES

Arroz con Queso 92

Asparagus and Cheese. 94

Bean and Corn Chili 184

Caponata 102

Chicken Fiesta Soup 192

Chicken Tortilla Soup 156

Corn on the Cob with Garlic
  Herb Butter 112

Country Sausage and Bean
  Soup. 48

Cran Orange Acorn Squash . . . 30

Creamy Curried Spinach. 96

Deluxe Potato Casserole 24

Donna's Potato Casserole 122

Escalloped Corn 109

Fiesta Black Bean Soup. 176

Herbed Fall Vegetables. 17

Macaroni and Cheese 194

Mediterranean Stew 84

Mexican Cheese Soup 154

Orange-Spiced Sweet
  Potatoes. 106

Parsnip and Carrot Soup 180

Pesto Rice and Beans 115

Polenta-Style Corn
  Casserole 71

Ratatouille with Garbanzo
  Beans. 72

Red Cabbage and Apples 112

Risi Bisi. 76

Index | **223**

Risotto-Style Peppered Rice ... 16

Roasted Tomato-Basil
Soup........................ 34

Scalloped Potatoes and
Parsnips 110

Scalloped Tomatoes and
Corn 31

Southwestern Corn and
Beans...................... 104

Spanish Paella-Style Rice...... 68

Spanish-Style Couscous....... 70

Spiced Apple & Cranberry
Compote 114

Spinach Gorgonzola Corn
Bread 96

Supper Squash Medley........ 98

Vegetable Curry 108

Wild Rice and Mushroom
Casserole.................. 100

Wild Rice with Fruit & Nuts..... 116

Winter Squash and Apples ... 120

Southwest Turkey Tenderloin
Stew.......................... 167

Southwestern Corn and
Beans 104

Southwestern Stuffed Peppers.. 206

Spanish Paella-Style Rice......... 68

Spanish-Style Couscous 70

Spiced Apple & Cranberry
Compote...................... 114

Spicy Fruit Dessert 12

Spicy Sweet & Sour
Mini-Franks 39

Spinach Gorgonzola Corn
Bread 96

Steamed Pumpkin Cake........ 142

Strawberry Rhubarb Crisp 128

Streusel Pound Cake 132

Stuffed Chicken Breasts 32

Super Slow Sloppy Joes 188

Supper Squash Medley 98

Sweet & Saucy Ribs 197

Tarragon Turkey & Pasta 178

Thai Chicken 54

The Best Beef Stew 202

Three-Bean Turkey Chili 164

Triple Chocolate Fantasy........ 208

Triple Delicious Hot Chocolate .. 204

TURKEY

Fresh Herbed Turkey Breast ... 46

Simple Turkey Soup 170

Southwest Turkey Tenderloin
Stew 167

Tarragon Turkey & Pasta 178

Three-Bean Turkey Chili 164

Turkey and Macaroni.......... 214

Turkey with Pecan-Cherry
Stuffing 26

Turkey and Macaroni............ 214

Turkey with Pecan-Cherry
Stuffing 26

Vegetable Curry 108

"Wake Up to Health" Cereal..... 200

Wild Mushroom Beef Stew........ 40

Wild Rice and Mushroom
Casserole 100

Wild Rice with Fruit & Nuts 116

Winter Squash and Apples 120